EFFECTIVE DIFFICULT CONVERSATIONS

EFFECTIVE DIFFICULT
CONVERSATIONS

A Step-by-Step Guide

CATHERINE B. SOEHNER *and* ANN DARLING

An imprint of the American Library Association
Chicago 2017

CATHERINE B. SOEHNER is the associate dean for research and user services at the J. Willard Marriott Library at the University of Utah. She received her master of library science degree from Indiana University and has held leadership positions in libraries since 1998.

ANN DARLING is the assistant vice president of undergraduate studies, and an associate professor in the Communication Department at the University of Utah. She has a master's degree (University of New Mexico) and a PhD in communication (University of Washington) and has been in leadership positions in higher education since 1996.

CATHERINE AND ANN have provided presentations on "effective difficult conversations" as part of the University of Utah Leadership Development Program since March 2013. The success of their presentation broadened their reach across campus and they began providing the same presentation for the Health Sciences Leadership Development Program for a total of four presentations each year.

© 2017 by the American Library Association

Extensive effort has gone into ensuring the reliability of the information in this book; however, the publisher makes no warranty, express or implied, with respect to the material contained herein.

ISBNs
978-0-8389-1495-3 (paper)
978-0-8389-1526-4 (PDF)
978-0-8389-1527-1 (ePub)
978-0-8389-1528-8 (Kindle)

Library of Congress Cataloging in Publication Control Number: 2016038069

Book design by Alejandra Diaz. Images © Shutterstock, Inc.

⊗ This paper meets the requirements of ANSI/NISO Z39.48–1992 (Permanence of Paper).

Printed in the United States of America
21 20 19 18 17   5 4 3 2 1

To anyone who patiently listened
while I talked about writing this book,
especially my husband, my number-one fan,
whose constant support allowed me to find the time
and perseverance to write this book.
~ CATHERINE

To all our workshop participants over the years
who helped us refine our thoughts and hear new questions.
~ ANN

CONTENTS

ACKNOWLEDGMENTS

I WOULD LIKE TO ACKNOWLEDGE THE INFLUENCE AND ASSISTANCE OF a few people who helped with the shaping of many of the ideas in this book.

When I took on my first leadership role as the head of the Science and Engineering Library at the University of California, Santa Cruz, I had the good fortune to work with Kate McGirr, who was the assistant university librarian for administrative services at that time. After I took on this new role, she met with me weekly to discuss every personnel issue I encountered and gave me the beginning skills I needed to hold difficult conversations.

Upon my arrival at the University of Utah I met Julianne Hinz, whose job I was taking over as she made plans for her retirement. Juli introduced me to several books on organizational psychology and appreciative inquiry and became a source of support during my first five years at this new institution. I also had the great fortune to meet Melanie Hawks, the organizational development manager at the J. Willard Marriott Library, who in addition to encouraging me to write this book, introduced me to the writings of Douglas Stone and Sheila Heen, Barry Oshry, and several others. These books have broadened my understanding of human nature and communication.

Of course, this book would not have happened without meeting my colleague and coauthor, Ann Darling. Our combined approaches are the backbone of all the steps in this book and reflect our different experiences and perspectives, which serve to balance the approaches we recommend. I have deep respect for her insights and judgment and have learned a lot from her as we worked together on this project over the past four years.

Finally, I am deeply grateful to my husband, who patiently read and reread many drafts of this book, offering a valuable outsider's perspective and feedback. His detail-oriented mind encouraged me to write better descriptions and examples to illustrate the concepts.

I am grateful for these influences on my life and career, without which this book would not have been possible.

~CATHERINE

Given my three degrees in communication, I have had literally dozens of teachers whose patience and wisdom are reflected in the pages of this book. I wish I could name them all but since I cannot, I want to give thanks to the following people who have shaped how I learned to think about communication: Lawrence Rosenfeld, Jean Civikly, Bob Shrag, Dick Jensen, Ann Staton, and Gerry Philipsen. In these pages you will learn about the importance of a 3×5 card and that coaching came to me directly from Jody Nyquist.

With about twenty years of administrative service, I also have a lot of mentors to acknowledge. These are colleagues who helped me see administration as a way to make a unique and valuable contribution to the institution. And because there is no way to make a contribution through administration without learning about difficult conversations, their voices can be heard throughout this book. Again, there are far too many individuals to name but a few must be: Tom Scheidel, Robert Newman, Robert Avery, Richard Rieke, and Louise Degn.

And then, of course, there are the people who are on my team no matter what endeavor currently captures my attention. These are friends and colleagues whose fingerprints are on everything I do, including this book. These people must be named: Martha Bradley-Evans, Deanna Dannels, and my parents, David and Mary Darling.

Finally, I acknowledge my coauthor, Catherine Soehner, without whom this book would never have happened. I have appreciated learning her stories, hearing her wisdom, and expanding my understanding of all the many ways that we become more human through our connections with others.

~ANN

INTRODUCTION

WE'VE ALL BEEN THERE.

At some point in our work life, whether as a new employee or as someone who is coming up to their twenty-five-year anniversary, we have all confronted that most dreaded of situations: the "difficult" conversation. Examples from all rungs of the organization ladder are numerous. We take on a new leadership position and discover that the previous person in that position did not deal with certain personnel issues, that is, did not want to have those "difficult" conversations. In addition, we might find in our new leadership position people who are not fulfilling the requirements of their positions, or others who are regularly negative or who bully people, and still others who are frequently late for their shift.

Then there are others of us who are not in leadership positions, but "difficult" conversations still loom on the horizon like a dreaded black cloud. For example, one of our colleagues is consistently humming or singing to themselves down the hallway; or another colleague has sent us an angry e-mail in response to something we said or did, which was not at all intended to offend, but offense was taken nevertheless. In order to keep on working with this person, you will need to clear up this misunderstanding, that is, have a "difficult" conversation.

We are confronted with "difficult" conversations everywhere. It is bad enough that we have these conversations in our personal life, but we probably need to have as many if not more in our work life. And unlike in our personal life, most of these conversations will have to be with people we may not particularly like and who might not like us. So what is a person to do?

Whether you are conflict-avoidant and terrified of having a "difficult" conversation or think of yourself as someone who can be blunt and "tell it like it is," this book has something to offer you. A successful and professional leader is one who is capable of managing all of the situations described above in a manner that is both compassionate and direct in order to create an effective conversation and a working solution, that is, an effective "difficult" conversation. This book will focus on having effective "difficult" conversations in your work life. It is not a self-help book, and it makes no claims to be able to solve all problems, either professional or personal. Some of the ideas and concepts presented here may sound familiar if you have already read other books dealing with this subject, especially books designed to make you a better listener using techniques of "active listening" and other aspects of good communication behaviors. However, it is our hope that this book will bring something new to the discussion while focusing on having "difficult" conversations in your professional life. The examples and settings will come from relatable work experiences and, in the end, it is our hope that your work life will become a little less stressful and a little more successful.

We frequently offer ourselves excuses for not dealing with personnel issues: since tenured colleagues cannot be easily fired, and unionized workers cannot be easily disciplined, why bother doing anything at all? Alternatively, maybe we say to ourselves, "It is necessary to go along to get along." Perhaps the excuse is as simple as "don't rock the boat," and it is easier just to maintain the status quo. However, these excuses are just that: excuses for not being the successful, dynamic, compassionate, and courageous professionals that we are meant to be. We hope that this book will help you achieve the level of courage needed to face each of these situations and many more.

To begin, it is necessary to define what we mean by a "difficult" conversation, and explain why, up until now, there have been quotation marks around the word "difficult." Unfortunately, the idea of what is a "difficult" conversation is not easily answered, which is why the entire first chapter of this book is devoted to defining a "difficult" conversation. As mentioned above, a difficult conversation is different for a conflict-avoidant person than for someone who likes to "tell it like it is." However, in both instances, as well as many others, there are some commonalities, which we discuss and highlight in chapter 1, as well as throughout the rest of the book. Suffice it to say, defining what is a difficult conversation is only the beginning of the discussion. The remaining chapters go on to discuss all aspects of your work life and how to make it more successful and more enjoyable.

Chapters 2, 3, and 4 focus on preparation. Thorough preparation is critical to having effective difficult conversations. Initially you might read these chapters and find yourself a little overwhelmed by the amount of time and attention devoted to preparation. This is purposeful. We think it is important that you understand the kind of work that goes into preparing for a difficult conversation. We also reassure you that over time some of these steps will become instinctual and the amount of time that you spend preparing for a difficult conversation will lessen, somewhat.

In chapter 2 we take the first of three steps in preparing for a difficult conversation: getting clear. Therefore, in order to have an effective difficult conversation, you need to self-reflect: this entails looking at yourself, the other person, and the situation with an objective, dispassionate, and thoughtful eye. Getting clear and being objective, thoughtful, and dispassionate about the other person and the situation are a necessary first step to having a productive difficult conversation. We discuss the practical aspects of whether this is a conversation you need to have, and how and when you need to have it.

In chapter 3 we discuss the next step in preparing for a difficult conversation: gathering any resources that might be helpful. The sole purpose of gathering resources is to make sure that the facts you have about the situation are as complete and accurate as possible. Our experience has taught us that giving insufficient attention to this step in the preparation process can result in ineffective difficult conversations. If you get the facts of the situation incorrect, you may spend a majority of the conversation debating your version of the situation versus the other person's version. This chapter describes the printed and human resources that might be helpful to consult before scheduling a difficult conversation.

In chapter 4 we discuss the last step in preparing for a difficult conversation: clarifying your message. Every productive difficult conversation is guided by a clear message that you need the other person to hear and understand. In this chapter we help you articulate a clear, succinct, direct, and compassionate message that you can use to guide a difficult conversation.

In chapter 5 we focus on the heart of the conversation. After carefully preparing for the conversation, it is equally important to consider what you will say during the conversation and, even more importantly, when and how you will respond to what the other person says.

In chapter 6 we give you the tools to hold yourself and others accountable. It all comes down to documentation: without documentation, it will be as if the conversation never happened; and considering the amount of time you have already given this process, you want to make sure that work turns into positive action. We call this next step "Write It Down." And this step is crucial to a difficult conversation's ultimate success.

In chapter 7 we encourage you to keep up regular meetings and continue to write up the results of those meetings. We title it "Keep up the Good Work," which probably says it all.

We address the issue of having difficult conversations with coworkers in chapter 8. There are unique aspects to these conversations that required a separate chapter to adjust the steps to manage the special relationship between coworkers.

In chapter 9 we use the tools described in earlier chapters in the context of change management. Learning how to help people through strategic planning and reorganization is imperative to a successful reorganization or change, and will most likely require many difficult conversations.

In chapter 10 we talk about a very important category of difficult conversations: those that are initiated by an employee who needs to talk to their supervisor about any number of issues, such as asking for a pay raise, a promotion, a new job assignment, or voicing concerns about management decisions that affect work assignments. We call it "Managing Up—How to Have Difficult Conversations with Your Boss."

Finally, we offer you our conclusion and some final thoughts. However, one important item of note is that both authors have botched most of the difficult conversations they had at the beginning of their supervisory careers. It was the recognition of this failure and a true desire to be successful leaders that led both of them in different institutions to develop methods for effective difficult conversations. Once you have identified an area where you need to improve, we recommend that you dive into that area with enthusiasm, read every article and book you can find on the topic, consult with others in similar positions, and begin to implement small improvements. This book is the result of both of us tackling an area where we admitted failure. It is also a reflection of the courage to admit that failure, and a documentation of our resilience.

Ultimately, this book provides you with step-by-step instructions on having difficult conversations, particularly in the workplace. We use real examples from our experiences as leaders in libraries and in higher education to illuminate the instructions, along with opportunities for you to reflect on your own situations. We know that by following these steps, you will gain confidence, courage, and a sense of integrity. We wish you great success as you approach each situation and we hope there will be a day when you no longer dread these conversations but look at them as new opportunities to learn more about yourself and how others see themselves in the world. It's an exciting and fascinating journey!

CHAPTER ONE

Difficult Conversations Defined

IN THIS CHAPTER WE DEFINE DIFFICULT CONVERSATIONS AND discuss what makes them difficult. We give you encouragement to have these conversations despite any hesitancy you might have. And if you are a person who jumps into these conversations without much thought, we encourage reflection to make these conversations effective. You are about to begin an exciting journey.

DEFINITION

The key word in the term *difficult conversation* is "difficult." What is a "difficult" conversation? That depends entirely on the individual. For a person who is conflict-avoidant, for example, a difficult conversation is any conversation that you have anxiety about, that worries you, or that you have put off, and where you are pretty certain the other person will not like what you are about to say. On the other hand, for a person who might be a "tell it like it is" person, a straight shooter who is not afraid to confront people, a difficult conversation may become one in which, after "telling it like it is," the other person becomes hostile, combative, or worse. What was a difficult conversation, entered into without reflection, has now turned into a difficult situation with a "difficult" employee, and it may only go downhill from there.

Thus, what is difficult is in the eye of the beholder, or rather, the mouth of the speaker. However, some generalizations and common examples can be given. For the authors, typical difficult conversations include the following.

💬 Telling someone they will not be rehired or they did not get the promotion they applied for.

Hiring, firing, and promoting employees are among the core elements of many leaders' portfolios. Hiring and promoting can be rewarding and even pleasurable conversations to have; and firing or denying promotions can be among the most difficult. Unfortunately, our jobs are filled with the give-and-take of this hiring cycle, and so thinking about how to manage the less pleasurable conversations is important.

There are many reasons why a leader might have to let someone go. When grant funding for a position ends and there are no other funds to continue the position, we have to let people go. This is an unfortunate reality of grant-funded projects. Back in 2008 and 2009, when the bottom dropped out of the American economy, many libraries faced major budget cuts that resulted in people losing their jobs. Sometimes we have to let people go because they are not performing their job adequately. Often the decision to let someone go happens after a long series of difficult conversations; if you have followed the advice given in chapter 6 this final difficult conversation will be made a little easier because it will not come as a complete shock to the employee. But if you have not been consistent about having frequent conversations and creating documentation, then letting someone go can be a terribly difficult process. These are conversations that have a huge impact on the lives of those with whom we work and are truly among the most difficult conversations we will have.

Similarly, telling someone that they did not get a promotion or a position they applied for will also prove to be a difficult conversation. Often people who have applied for a promotion have worked with you in the unit for quite some time. The employee may have become a personal friend and trusted colleague. In these instances, difficult conversations have an added layer of personal complication that must be considered.

Both of us have had the responsibility of letting someone go and each conversation was as unique as the circumstances. Letting go of a very popular teacher resulted in a large group of angry students descending on the chair of the department's office. Informing a staff member that the funds supporting her position would not be renewed brought tears and a few slammed doors. These are the realities of doing leadership in an academic environment.

💬 **Telling someone they are not performing adequately.**

Like hiring, firing and promoting, performance reviews are a regular part of a leader's job. In many libraries and other academic units, we are expected to conduct performance reviews on an annual basis. We would like to report that their regularity makes them easier but that would not be true. For most of us, these conversations are especially difficult precisely because of their regularity and because we are conducting them with people that we may have come to know quite well.

Negative performance reviews are especially tricky because the task is to clearly identify the behavior that needs to be changed while also motivating the employee to stay engaged and be willing to improve. Hiring new employees is almost always more expensive and time-consuming than training and supporting the employees currently on staff. So finding a way to conduct this conversation effectively is critical to your success as a leader.

These conversations can be especially difficult if the other person believes they are doing an excellent job. However, avoiding telling someone that they are not meeting expectations is both unkind and unfair. How can anyone improve their performance unless we tell them that they are not meeting expectations? While you can put off having the difficult conversation, wait until their yearly review, and then surprise them with a poor performance review, that practice would be highly discouraged by any Human Resources professional. It is unfair and unkind not to help them improve before the year-end review simply because you want to avoid a difficult conversation. Furthermore, ignoring the poor performance of employees can affect the morale of those performing well. It can be demoralizing to work hard every day only to see others making a minimal effort with minimal or no consequences.

You will read several examples of performance reviews that went well and some that went poorly. These are probably some of the more frequent conversations you will have.

💬 Telling someone you need them to do something they don't want to do, or telling someone you need them to stop doing something that they like to do or feel entitled to do.

These types of conversations may be less formal in terms of institutional norms but they are no less difficult. Especially in academic settings like libraries, most of us have benefited from the opportunity to "own" our jobs and "make them our own." This privilege can make working in an academic setting rewarding. Unfortunately, sometimes we forget that this opportunity to create our own work is a privilege and not a right. We often forget, as well, that all working situations change; new tasks get assigned and new technologies demand that old tasks be done in new ways. Redirecting people's work is a common, if less formal, aspect of a leader's job.

These two situations are one of the few that apply equally to managers and coworkers. Managers are often faced with the unenviable task of telling someone to do something or to stop doing something. These conversations are inherently difficult because, by definition, the person you are telling to change may not immediately want to hear it. So whether you, the manager, are conflict-avoidant or someone who does not hesitate to tell it like it is, if not handled with some level of reflection and planning this conversation is not likely to go well. Similarly, an employee on any level in the organization may need to have a difficult conversation with a coworker who is doing something you would like them to stop doing, like interrupting you when you are trying to work; or asking them to do something they don't want to do, like closing their office door when they take a phone call.

We have had the experiences of telling a colleague they will no longer be fulfilling an administrative role as well as asking someone to teach a class on a day or time outside of their usual teaching schedule. These conversations are essential to the efficient functioning of a unit and they are often quite complicated.

COMPONENTS OF A DIFFICULT CONVERSATION

There are a number of reasons why we might hesitate to have a difficult conversation. Many of us just simply do not like conflict in any form and would prefer not to hold any conversation where the other person might not like what we have to say. We have been calling this type of person "conflict-avoidant."

Below are some common reasons why someone who is conflict-avoidant might consider a conversation "difficult." These are also some common reasons, especially the last one, why someone who doesn't mind confronting people and "telling it like it is" might hesitate because they could turn a blunt conversation into a difficult situation.

💬 **The other person might react badly (anger, emotion, tears, retribution).**

People, being humans, react to information that they don't want to hear with a wide range of emotions. We've heard stories of managers who were cursed at in a very loud voice by a colleague after the latter had learned that his tenure case received a negative vote. And we've heard stories of colleagues attempting to build coalitions against the supervisor when a merit review didn't result in the raise they'd hoped for. It is true that these difficult conversations can result in heated emotions expressed without restraint; but it is also true that often the fears are worse than the realities. These reactions from the other person are awkward at best and frightening at worst. Using the process outlined in this book can reduce these reactions significantly.

💬 **You might be rejected (by the individual and their friends).**

Let's be honest, none of us likes to be rejected, and most of us want to be accepted and loved. Risking rejection is something most of us avoid at all costs. It is also true, however, that being a leader means that occasionally you will have to risk rejection.

One of the most important things to learn is that as a leader you will be required to regard your friendships differently. As a supervisor or as a coworker you still need to work with people, and their friends, with whom you will have to have difficult conversations. You may need something from them in the future, or you may just not want them to shun you in day-to-day interactions. These are natural fears and they must be managed. You will be called to treat your friends as employees, even when that is very difficult.

💬 **You might do it badly and make things worse.**

Even for a person who is ready to enter into conflict, this concern is a very real one. As you will read in the next section, there are high stakes involved in hosting a difficult conversation and the consequences and impact of an *ineffective* difficult conversation are very real. The consequences can range from a lawsuit to lost trust and maybe some banged-up furniture. Having a plan to address a difficult conversation will do a lot to reduce this particular concern whether you are conflict-avoidant or not.

THE BAD NEWS AND THE GOOD NEWS

While we are thrilled to have the opportunity to share our thoughts on and experiences with having effective difficult conversations, we think it is very important to make one thing perfectly clear. *No matter what you do to prepare, these conversations are never easy and they can be terribly difficult.* As we have described earlier in this chapter, there is a lot at stake in these types of conversations. In fact, it is not hyperbolic to state that often these conversations are focused on the highest of stakes in our working relationships. Telling someone that grant funds have expired and they will not be rehired is tantamount to telling them that they will not be able to pay their rent or feed their children. Telling someone that they are not performing their tasks adequately is often heard as telling someone they are an inadequate human being. Very high stakes indeed! In fact, one of the authors was once told by a mentor that "the day you think these conversations are easy is probably the day that you should get out of administration." Wise words. Our recommendation is that you go into each difficult conversation assuming that the stakes are even higher than is evident on the surface.

The good news is that *these conversations can be prepared for.* That's why we are sharing this book with you. There is abundant evidence from research and experience that there is a set of practical steps and learnable skills that can be brought to bear on these conversations. Steps like adequate preparation, including extensive consultation, are quite important in the context of having effective difficult conversations. Steps like careful follow-up can ensure that effective difficult conversations result in desirable behavioral change and accountability for both the employee and yourself. Communication skills like listening and nonverbal immediacy and clear messages can go a long way toward making difficult conversations effective. We hope this book helps you plan for those steps and begin to build those skills. Like all skills, though, reflective practice is strongly advised.

The even better news is that these *conversations can be productive.* Difficult conversations can yield important behavior change. People that we supervise, armed with clear expectations and supported by clear and compassionate messages when those expectations are not met, can transform into model employees. Through difficult conversations we might learn what is keeping an employee from performing adequately and might be able to put supportive structures in place so that performance can meet expectations. Through difficult conversations we might discover alternative ways to support an individual whose grant funding has expired. There is much to be learned through a carefully navigated difficult conversation.

And the news gets even better. We believe, and our experience confirms, that by having these conversations *you will gain confidence, strength, and integrity.* A great irony of life as a manager is that avoiding difficult conversations makes the work much more difficult. Tasks don't get completed on time and at the right level of quality. People can be confused and unhappy, which can make for low morale. We believe, and the argument we hope this book helps us to make, that the difference between a minimally successful manager and a truly successful one is the capacity for having effective difficult conversations. We argue that you will be remembered and promoted not because you manage your budget well and meet deadlines, although these are very important, but because you help the people around you reach, and maybe exceed, their professional potential. Even though having these difficult conversations may never be easy, we believe that if you commit yourself to following the steps identified in this book and developing the communication skills we suggest, you will become confident in your abilities and feel satisfied that there is integrity in the way that you interact with those under your supervision.

ACTIVITY

Take a few minutes to think about a difficult conversation that you are facing.

- Write down the context and the facts about the situation. Write down as many details as come to mind. Who is involved? What do you know or feel about the person? What do you want this person to do or change? What do you need to tell them? What is their relationship to you? What are the unique parts of the overall situation that make it complicated?

- Write down your concerns about having the conversation and what might make you hesitate to have the conversation. Be explicit and thorough here.

We hope you will use the details that you have recorded here to apply the concepts that we present in the rest of the book. Doing that may help anchor your learning and prepare you to have this difficult conversation in an effective way.

CHAPTER TWO

Getting Clear

AS DISCUSSED ABOVE IN CHAPTER 1, DIFFICULT CONVERSATIONS are different for everyone. Each situation is different, each person having the conversation is different, and therefore no two conversations will be the same. Despite this, we identify steps that you can take before, during, and after a difficult conversation that are applicable in almost all situations requiring you to have a difficult conversation. In this chapter, we take the first of three steps in preparing for a difficult conversation: getting clear.

What do we mean by "getting clear"? Getting clear is the thought process and perhaps even soul-searching one needs to do before having a difficult conversation. Probably the best term to use is "self-reflection." What kind of self-reflection are we talking about? We did indicate in our introduction that this is not a self-help book. Therefore, you might ask, "Why do I need to self-reflect before a difficult conversation? After all, the problem is with the other person. If anyone needs to self-reflect, it is the employee who is causing problems and not doing their job. They are the ones who should self-reflect on why they are screwing up." This is a legitimate question, and it may explain why having a conversation with the other person is so difficult. This question reveals a lot of feelings, assumptions, judgments, and resentments that make a conversation difficult. Therefore, in order to have an effective difficult conversation, we invite you to self-reflect: this entails looking at yourself, the other person, and the situation with an objective, dispassionate, and thoughtful eye. Getting clear and being objective, thoughtful, and dispassionate about the other person and the situation are necessary first steps to having an effective difficult conversation.

We cannot overstate the importance of getting clear. In our experience, initiating a difficult conversation before getting clear can result in an ineffective and often unpleasant conversation. In this chapter, we introduce four key questions, the answers to which will help you get clear. In addition, we explain why the answers to these four questions are important, and we help you develop responses to them. Getting clear helps you develop the internal confidence you need to go forward with your conversation.

💬 Why do you need to have this conversation at all?

In general, we advocate not having difficult conversations unless they are absolutely necessary. There are many benefits to not having a difficult conversation. Having difficult conversations is always risky and taxing no matter how well prepared you are. They are definitely time-consuming when you consider the preparation and follow-up necessary for effective difficult conversations. You always run the risk of the situation becoming worse. Having too many difficult conversations, and engaging in them too frequently, can have a negative effect on the goodwill that you need to be an effective leader. One of the most important "tips" we give you in this book is never to have a difficult conversation that you don't need to have. Reflecting on this question—why you need to have this conversation at all—can help you step away from conversations that you do not need to have.

In addition, reflecting on this first question is important because it invites you to imagine how the situation might evolve if you don't ever have this difficult conversation. There are some situations that require difficult conversations: addressing illegal activity, workplace violence, and discrimination, for example. If your reflection leads you to believe that the behavior will continue undeterred, then you have your answer and should feel quite confident that you need to have this conversation.

Finally, reflecting on this first question is important because every once in a while you find yourself in a situation that has the potential of resolving itself. Perhaps the person with whom you need to have this conversation is looking for another position and has become a finalist; in that case, it would be good to delay the conversation. Alternatively, it could be that the person has become alert to the signals that others are sending them and has begun to correct their own behavior because of peer pressure. Therefore, sometimes putting off a difficult conversation will allow the situation to get resolved on its own. Sometimes people, on their own, correct their behavior or find another way to resolve the issue. While we normally do not advocate procrastination, every now and then putting off a difficult conversation and watching the situation from afar can be a productive tactic.

💬 Why do you need to have this conversation?

This is the second question you need to ask yourself in order to get clear. When you reflect dispassionately and objectively on the answer to this question, you should be able to determine whether you need to have the difficult conversation that you have been dreading. If you determine upon reflection that you do need to have the conversation, the self-reflective work you put into answering the question will help make the difficult conversation more effective.

The answer to this question is not as simple as you might think. At first blush, the answer may seem obvious: of course you need to have this conversation. You are the boss, there is a problem, and clearly, you need to solve it. However, sometimes in leadership positions you begin to think that *every* conflict or problematic situation is yours to address. Therefore, it is easy to see why you might begin to think this way. Many days your calendar is full of people who want to tell you what isn't working and let you know how you should fix it. Your e-mail is often full of issues that need to be dealt with and a litany of descriptions about how the world is falling apart on your watch. However, careful reflection on this second question, that is, why do *you* need to have this conversation, often reveals that, in fact, not every conflict is yours to resolve and every issue is not under your direct influence.

There are a number of ways to reflect and get clear on this question. Sometimes difficult conversations are guided by policy. People in certain positions are responsible, according to policy, for having some types of difficult conversations. Issues of terminating or changing conditions of employment, for example, are often dictated by policy, as are conversations that might lead to formal disciplinary actions. Therefore, one way to get clear on the answer to this question is to ask, "Does policy require that I, in particular, have this conversation?"

If policy does not help you get clear on the answer to this question, then you are faced with some deeper reflections. Often it is useful to think about another set of questions: "Am I directly affected by or involved in the issue that is triggering this difficult conversation?" and "Is there someone *else* who should have this conversation?" We advise, for the most part, that if you are not directly involved in the issue, then it is possible that you are not the person who should have this conversation. And remember, your default position should be *not* to have difficult conversations. As we stated above, difficult conversations are emotionally taxing and time-consuming, are risky and can make the situation worse, and, if done too frequently, can have a negative effect on your employees' goodwill.

The example we often use to illustrate this advice is the situation in which you as a supervisor have assigned two coworkers to work together on a project and they are not getting along. Perhaps one feels like the other is not pulling their weight. Perhaps one feels like the other is not listening to their great ideas. Regardless, the partnership is not progressing well and one of them has sought you out, as their supervisor, and asked you to talk to the other one. We would suggest that this is not *your* conversation to have. To reach this conclusion you need to ask yourself the three questions mentioned above: Does policy require that I have this conversation? Am I directly affected by or involved in the issue? And is there someone else who should have this conversation? The answer to these questions should lead you to determine that this is not your conversation to have: policy does not require you to have the conversation and you are not directly involved in the issue. If you still feel like you need to say something, either because you are the de facto leader, or that the tension between these two coworkers is generally making for an uncomfortable work environment; then the only conversation that you might have is to empower the one who has come to you to have the conversation themselves. You might suggest, "It sounds to me that there are some important things you need to discuss with your coworker. I know it will be a difficult conversation, but it is probably best that you talk to them rather than me since you are most directly involved."

Next, let us consider a situation when the conversation is one that you, as a supervisor, need to have. The three questions still apply: Does policy require that I have this conversation? Am I directly affected by or involved in the issue? And is there someone else who should have this conversation? As to the first question, policy dictates will apply to any number of situations. For example, if you are directly aware, or are made aware that certain things are occurring, such as an employee who is sexually harassing someone, stealing office equipment, or lying on their time sheet, policy dictates that you need to have this difficult conversation (or someone in Human Resources, depending on your institution's specific policy).

Similarly, if you are told that an employee who is one of your direct reports is coming late to work, or coming late to a shift, it is probably your conversation to have. We discuss in detail how to have these conversations in chapter 5. If an employee comes to you complaining about a coworker who is talking too loudly in an adjacent cubicle, or if an employee comes to you complaining that a coworker on a joint assignment is not doing their fair share, you can rightfully conclude that this is not your conversation to have initially. At the outset, it is the other employee's conversation to have, and it is your job to help them with it by suggesting that they talk to the other person and see if it cannot be resolved between the two of them. However, if the employee states that they already have had the conversation, or comes back to you after having the conversation and reports that nothing has changed, then you have some choices to make: you can continue to coach the employee to engage in difficult conversations to bring about resolution or you can direct the employee to a campus resource that specializes in mediation such as an ombudsman or a Human Resources specialist. We suggest not attempting to do this mediation yourself.

As for complaints about the work environment, such as a complaint about coworkers leaving the break room a mess, we have stated above that these are not conversations employees need to have. However, they are not necessarily conversations you as a supervisor need to have either, since it is not controlled by policy and it may not directly affect you. Since there is no one else who should have this conversation, that is, the third question, then it is our opinion that it is best left for a group conversation that you, as a supervisor, can facilitate. This way no one has to have a one-on-one difficult conversation, but instead can conduct a group conversation that could resolve the issue through general agreement.

Let us consider an example involving a supervisor that illustrates many of the points we have discussed. Roberta, a department chair, supervises six librarians. One librarian, Iris, sent what she thought was an innocuous e-mail to Maria, another librarian. Maria sent back what appeared to be an angry e-mail. Maria had used a "?!" at the end of the Subject line, which seemed to indicate anger. Iris brought the e-mail to Roberta to complain that Maria frequently had angry responses to simple requests and demanded that Roberta do something.

Roberta began by considering the three questions posed above: Does policy require that I have this conversation? Am I directly affected by or involved in the issue? Is there someone else who should have this conversation? Policy did not require that Roberta engage in this conversation. Furthermore, Roberta was not directly involved in the issue, Iris was. Finally, there was someone else who should have this conversation, namely Iris. This was Iris's conversation to have. As the conversation continued between Iris and Roberta, Roberta provided coaching so that Iris felt more confident about having the conversation with Maria directly.

Let's consider a situation presented to a supervisor where it is their conversation to have. There was an instance where a young woman, Nina, asked to meet with Roberta, the department chair of a unit within a medium-sized library. Nina was not a direct report to Roberta, and was further down in the organizational chart. In that meeting Nina talked about her own supervisor, a man, who frequently complimented people, both men and women, on what they were wearing, such as, "That's a good looking shirt! Great color! Is that a new tie? Looking sharp!" As a young woman early in her career, Nina was uncomfortable when these comments were directed to her about her appearance and wanted her supervisor to compliment her work rather than what she was wearing. Roberta knew that this kind of exchange and Nina's feelings of discomfort could be seen as sexual harassment if left to continue without intervention. Sexual harassment claims have serious legal consequences and there are strict policies on how to handle them. The male supervisor, Mateo, was a direct report to Roberta. He was a wonderful colleague, full of good humor, resilient in the face of challenges, and always ready to take on a new idea. It was also well-known that Mateo provided compliments to everyone he met.

Roberta began by considering the three questions posed above: Does policy require that I have this conversation? Am I directly affected by or involved in the issue? And is there someone else who should have this conversation? Policy on sexual harassment does require that once made known, a supervisor needs to step in immediately. Though not directly affected by Mateo's behavior, in fact, Roberta genuinely enjoyed the compliments Mateo bestowed, and policy overruled the answer to this question, "Am I directly affected or involved in the issue?" Finally, Roberta wondered if Nina had taken the initiative to try to solve this herself. Roberta began with the question to Nina, "Have you said anything to Mateo about this?" Nina said that she had not and that she would be horribly uncomfortable saying anything. With a little more conversation, Nina thought she would have the courage to say something if Roberta was also in the room. This was Roberta's conversation to have.

As an important side note, Roberta decided that it would be best to pull Mateo aside first and give him a preview of the conversation. Roberta's experience of Mateo was that he was a good-natured and sensitive man and that it was highly unlikely that his intentions were about harassment. Roberta's individual conversation with Mateo allowed him to be upset that anyone would take anything he said in a bad way. By the time the three of them met later that afternoon, Mateo was more calm and was able to respond to Nina in a kind, gentle manner and agreed to stop his compliments about her appearance and focus on her work.

A final example of difficult conversations supervisors need to face deals with employees who go around their own boss to complain to a higher-level supervisor. They might come to you because you are their boss's boss. Such a conversation with Roberta as the department chair, Bill as one of her section leaders and a direct report, and Frieda as one of Bill's employees, could go something like this:

Frieda: Hi Roberta. Thanks for meeting with me. Did you know that Bill has completely changed how we do things down in reserves, and now everything is going to hell? We're not getting things done, and things are falling through the cracks. Do you think you could talk to him about it?

Roberta: It sounds like you are frustrated with the changes Bill made.

Frieda: I am! Things are falling through the cracks!

Roberta: There are a couple of issues I'm hearing. First, I am aware of the changes Bill made. We talk on a regular basis and he provided me with a plan for the changes and the advantages he believed would come as a result. Second, I'm wondering if you have examples of the things that are falling through the cracks.

Frieda: Well, yeah, I have examples.

Roberta: Have you presented those examples to Bill so that he better understands what your concerns are? If you have concrete examples of what is not working and potential solutions to those concerns, Bill will be in a better place to make adjustments.

Frieda: But if I talk to Bill, I just look like I'm complaining. He already doesn't like me. I just thought you would be interested in hearing how things are going. You always say your door is open.

Roberta: My door is open for conversations like this one. And, Bill will be better able to hear what the problem is if you provide him with specific examples and a potential solution for mitigating the problem. If you like, we can talk about what you might say to Bill so that you can feel prepared.

Frieda: So, what you're saying is that you don't want to get involved.

Roberta: I'm not saying that I don't want to get involved. I am saying that since you are the person closest to the issues, since you have at least one example and potential solutions, you are the best person to deliver the message.

This example illustrates three things of note: first, that just because an employee comes to you with a complaint about another employee, you don't always have to respond to it; and second, an "open door" policy does not always mean you have to conduct every difficult conversation that is presented to you. We cannot stress enough how important it is to minimize the number of difficult conversations you have, and therefore how important it is to make sure you go through the three questions we have presented to be certain that any potential difficult conversation is really yours to have. Finally, Roberta's last sentence is an excellent example of "contrasting," a tool described in detail in the book *Crucial Confrontations* (Patterson, Grenny, McMillan, and Switzler 2005, 94–95). Contrasting is a wonderful tool to use when someone interprets what we are saying differently than what was intended (94).

💬 Why do you need to have this conversation now?

A difficult conversation is a communication event and in the world of communication, timing is everything. Good news given during a difficult time can cheer people up, and bad news given at the end of a bad day can seem worse than it is. When people ask, "Do you want the good news first, or the bad news?" they are acknowledging that timing is everything. Chances are you have had the experience of reading an e-mail at the end of a day and reacting badly; you may have thought the e-mail was an affront or that the sender was implying that you hadn't completed a task according to specifications. But, being level-headed, you didn't respond. In the morning, after a full night of sleep, you reread the e-mail only to discover that nothing in your immediate interpretation was correct and that the sender was only asking for some additional information. Timing is incredibly important! Therefore, before having a difficult conversation you should ask yourself, "When should I have this difficult conversation: now, or later; Monday morning, or Friday afternoon; right away, or tomorrow?" Getting clear on the timing of a difficult conversation is the third question you need to consider.

Hattie and Timperley (2007) report that employees prefer feedback that occurs as close in time to the target behavior as possible. We know this is hard to do: if the conversation is going to be difficult, it is easy to put it off. However, there are reasons for having the conversation as soon as possible. One of the most obvious and practical reasons is that the behavior you need to address is disrupting work and causing problems. It may even rise to the level of legal necessity, if the behavior at issue involves workplace violence, discrimination, or sexual harassment. Another reason for having the conversation sooner rather than later is that letting the errant behavior go on without a signal or correction can create the impression that it isn't such a big deal; it can create the impression that you are not particularly concerned about this errant behavior. When you do decide to address the behavior, resentments about unclear or inconsistent guidance can get in the way of an effective conversation. Hence, we recommend trying to have the conversation as soon as possible.

That being said, our experience also tells us that there are some times that are better than other times for conversations like these. It can be tempting to have these conversations at the end of a week, maybe on a Friday, so that neither you nor the other person has to be in each other's presence in the days following a difficult conversation. As inviting as this option seems, we hope you will resist this temptation. Dropping difficult conversations at the end of the week rarely has the positive effect for which you are hoping. Most people are tired at the end of a workweek and people are rarely at their best on Friday afternoons. As a result, the employee rarely takes the opportunity to reflect and consider cool-headed responses. Instead, it is more likely that they will experience a deepening resentment and spend time complaining to their colleagues. Without any opportunity to follow up immediately with you, the individual may take the entire weekend to "stew" on the injustices and unresolved feelings that the conversation generated. They may even enlist some other coworkers to agree about the "unfairness" of the situation. Therefore, based on years of trying to have productive difficult conversations on Fridays or on the last workday before a holiday, we believe that it is much more productive to have the conversations in the beginning or middle of the week. This allows the other person time to ask follow-up questions, as well as time to ease through those awkward moments that are inevitable after a difficult conversation.

💬 How do you schedule this conversation?

Often we are asked, "How do you let someone know that you need to have a difficult conversation?" We recommend *not* letting the person know that you need to have a difficult conversation until you have moved through all of the preparatory steps that we discuss in chapters 2 through 4. Inevitably, as soon as you let someone know that you need to have a difficult conversation, they will want to have it immediately and, if you are not prepared, the conversation could go badly.

As you consider how to schedule a difficult conversation, we encourage you to use the tools at your disposal. For example, do you have regularly scheduled meetings with the person with whom you wish to speak? Can the conversation wait that long, or do you need to address the issue immediately? If you can use a regularly scheduled, one-on-one meeting to discuss the situation, the process should be relatively easy. If, however, you do not have a scheduled meeting coming up soon enough, you will need to schedule a meeting.

We recommend using either e-mail or a brief stop by the person's office to request that you both schedule an appointment to talk about the issues that have arisen. Let us consider the positives and negatives of using e-mail first. Many institutions have electronic calendaring systems used by everyone in the organization. If this is the case for you, use this tool to determine availability prior to sending an e-mail to schedule a time to meet. For example, if you need to schedule a difficult conversation with an employee who has started missing shift assignments, your e-mail could look something like this:

> Hi Joy,
> I need to talk with you about your service desk schedule. Our calendars suggest that 3:00 p.m. today is clear for both of us. I'll send a meeting invitation in just a few minutes. Please let me know if you can make that time. Thanks!

The positive aspect of using e-mail is that you don't have to interact with Joy face-to-face. She cannot start asking questions or demand to have the conversation immediately. The negative aspect of using e-mail is that Joy might write back and tell you that she forgot to update her calendar, and has a conflict at 3:00 p.m. Depending on your experience with Joy, this might be easy to fix in one or two more e-mails. However, if Joy likes to make a lot of excuses, you might need to stop by her office and set a specific time to meet.

Stopping by someone's office to ask for a meeting rather than using e-mail has some advantages. If stopping by someone's office to set a meeting is the typical culture of your library or if your office is in close proximity to the other person, you should consider using this technique. You might also choose to stop by someone's office because e-mail has been an ineffective way to schedule a meeting. In either case, you will need to be prepared for the other person to ask to have the conversation right at that moment rather than schedule a time. Normally, we recommend deferring to a scheduled time since it is better for both of you if a protected period of time has been established, rather than having a spontaneous conversation. A scheduled time allows you to have the conversation in the location of your choice, with no other distractions, and an opportunity to feel completely prepared. If the other person does ask to meet right away and you want to defer the conversation, consider using the following phrasing to move the conversation to a scheduled time:

> This is the kind of conversation that I want to make sure we've both been able to block out time for. What is the next opening on your calendar, and I'll do what I can to make that work for me.

A negative aspect of deferring the conversation is that the employee might become very distracted and unable to do their work as they worry about the conversation until you have the meeting. However, being prepared for the conversation on your end entirely outweighs the potential of a distracted employee.

If this other person is particularly difficult to schedule and the conversation is imperative to have right away, we recommend that you be completely ready to have the conversation when you stop by that person's office. The positive aspect of having the meeting right away is that the conversation will happen sooner rather than later. The negative aspect of having the conversation right then is that you might have the conversation in that person's office, which may have many distractions, like phones ringing and electronic indicators of messages. We do not recommend having a difficult conversation on the spur of the moment unless you are completely prepared.

Whether you request to have a meeting over e-mail or request a meeting through a brief stop by the office, it will be best if the conversation can happen within a day or two of the request to schedule an appointment. That way, there is less time for either of you to worry unnecessarily about the conversation. It is best, therefore, to make a request for a meeting at the beginning of the week rather than on a Friday so that neither of you has to think about the conversation over the weekend.

ACTIVITY

Reflecting on the concepts presented in chapter 2, write down answers to the following questions to get clear about your particular situation.

- Why do you need to have this conversation *at all*?
- Why do *you* need to have this conversation at all?
    - » Does policy require that I have this conversation?
    - » Am I directly affected by or involved in the issue?
    - » Is there someone else who should have this conversation?
- Why do you need to have this conversation *now*?
- How will you schedule this conversation?

CHAPTER THREE

Gathering Resources

ONCE YOU HAVE BECOME CLEAR THAT THIS IS A CONVERSATION you need to have, and how and when you need to have it (as discussed in chapter 2), it is time to take the next step. It is time to gather any resources that might be helpful. The sole purpose of gathering resources is to make sure that the facts you have about the situation are as complete and accurate as possible. As in the previous chapter, our experience has taught us that giving insufficient attention to this step in the preparation process can result in ineffective difficult conversations. If you get the facts incorrect, you will spend a majority of the conversation debating your version of the situation versus the other person's version. Having the facts can sidestep this minefield of debate. This chapter describes the printed and human resources that might be helpful to consult before scheduling a difficult conversation.

GATHER DOCUMENTATION

First, we invite you to consider any documentation that might be useful in helping you prepare for this conversation. It is always important to consider any history that this individual might have with either the behavior that you are trying to manage or the institution.

Some of the types of documentation that might be useful include the following:

1. A contract or letter of appointment. Were any agreements established in these documents that might have implications for the conversation that you need to have?
2. Any memos documenting disciplinary action. Has this individual been involved in conversations like these before? Is the same behavior at issue? What actions were taken then and how are those related to actions that you are considering now?
3. Documented leaves. Has this individual taken any personal or professional leaves? How long ago? Is it possible to know why those leaves were taken? Are those reasons connected to the behaviors that you are hoping to change?
4. Documentation regarding use of vacation and sick days. It can be important to be very certain of the ways in which the individual uses these institutional resources.
5. E-mail messages and meeting minutes. Were there any action items described in meeting minutes that this person has put off? Were there agreements made that are being disregarded? Are there e-mails that demonstrate a negative behavior that you want to address?

Let's consider the situation of Roberta, who had a long-term situation with a particularly difficult post-tenure review. In the university that employed Roberta, librarian faculty are reviewed every five years once tenure has been obtained. Once the review is complete, it is policy that the chair of the department will have a discussion with the person undergoing the five-year, post-tenure review about the results. As a brand new chair, Roberta had to have a conversation to talk about a negative post-tenure review with Sue, a librarian faculty member that she supervised. In the initial conversation, Roberta did not address this step, that is, gathering documentation, in the preparation process. Roberta did not read Sue's previous post-tenure review reports and so the conversation that Roberta had with Sue was superficial and ineffective. Because Roberta did not consult previous documentation, she was unable to notice and talk about the consistent pattern of poor job performance which led to an ineffective difficult conversation. No behavior change resulted and a clear record of consistent poor performance was not created. As we will discuss in a moment, failing to consult previous documentation was one of two types of resources that Roberta failed to consider; and, as we have been warning, any ineffective difficult conversation is likely to be repeated, often with higher stakes. The next time Sue was up for a post-tenure review, Roberta was more prepared but the issues had also magnified.

CONSULT OTHER PEOPLE

Second, we invite you to consider other people who might be consulted. Chief among the people that we recommend you consult is your Human Resources representative. It is never, ever too early to consult your Human Resources representative. They will have a host of other resources at their disposal that can be of service to you. They will have also, almost always, dealt with a situation like the one you are facing. This experience allows them to give good advice about other documentation that you might consider, language that you might use in setting up the appointment for the difficult conversation, and other individuals you might consult for help. They are required to maintain confidentiality, unless it is a situation of sexual harassment, or you or the other person are a danger to yourself or others. Additionally, if the situation that you are facing becomes more serious and ultimately results in disciplinary action, your Human Resources individual will be a great partner at every step in the process. Chapters 6 and 7 address preparation for disciplinary action in more detail and working with your Human Resources professionals as a team.

We also recommend, where reasonable, consulting other individuals for ideas and support. Of course, where personnel matters are concerned, utmost care must be taken to address appropriate concerns for privacy and confidentiality. But often it can be helpful to consult mentors, others who hold your position in the institution or in other institutions. Sometimes it is even useful to consult people who have been in your organization or unit for a long time and have some institutional wisdom that might be helpful. Again, when consulting individuals outside of the realm of Human Resources, it is vital to respect issues of privacy and confidentiality; resist any temptation to consult with someone, even a dear friend, who cannot be trusted to keep your confidence.

CONSULT YOURSELF

Finally, before having a difficult conversation you also must consult yourself. Difficult conversations always have an emotional undertone and these undertones can become quite destructive if you have not done a healthy and deep reflection about any personal connections or history with this individual. If we are being honest, many of us tend to dislike people who complain a lot, who are bullies, know-it-alls, or who like to appear superior to others. Reflecting on these connections or histories can help you develop a full profile of the undertones that might be at play in the difficult conversation for which you are preparing. For example, John, an employee you supervise, tends to be loud when he talks and he frequently complains about things over which no one has any control. When preparing for a difficult conversation with John about his request for new resources during a tight budget year, you might be tempted to deny his request just because it's John who is asking. If you would normally provide the resources to another person who is more likeable, then you should provide those same resources to John. Imagining John as someone you like will help you to do that.

Returning to the example of the difficult post-tenure review case, Roberta also failed to complete this step of self-reflection. One of the reasons that the former reports were not consulted is that the new chair and the individual had a particularly powerful personal history early on in both of their careers; this personal history was not considered prior to the conversation and this prevented the new chair from fully preparing for the situation. Prior to becoming the department chair, Roberta and Sue were equal colleagues and good friends. When Roberta was going through a divorce, Sue was welcoming, kind, and provided very helpful advice. Now, ten years later, Roberta was promoted to department chair and Sue reported to her directly. Additionally, Sue was going through a particularly difficult time in her own life, which included a drug-addicted son and the recent loss of a dear pet. Roberta failed to reflect on the guilt she felt about having to deliver this bad news to a person who was going through a tough time and who had treated her so kindly earlier in her career. Because she didn't reflect on this guilt she was unable to put it aside and realize that their personal past was not relevant to the current task. Roberta's initial difficult conversation was superficial and ineffective both because of a lack of attention to the history of poor performance and because her unconscious guilt prevented her from being as clear and direct as she needed to be in this conversation.

But an ineffective difficult conversation will almost always lead to a second opportunity. During Sue's next post-tenure review, the faculty review committee evaluating her case again drew very strong conclusions that Sue was not performing up to the standards of a tenured colleague. Now Roberta had to face having another difficult conversation with Sue and this time she was determined to be better prepared.

After considering the questions in chapter 2 and getting clear that this really was Roberta's conversation to have, both because policy dictated it and she was Sue's supervisor, Roberta decided to use one of her regular meetings with Sue to address the results of the post-tenure review. As Roberta began to improve in the area of holding difficult conversations, she was able to recognize the importance of documentation. As you might expect, since the initial conversation of the review described above did not go well, Sue continued her pattern of poor performance. This gave Roberta a second chance. In the next conversation about a negative post-tenure review, Roberta gathered documentation, including several previous post-tenure reviews, annual teaching evaluations, the record of publication and creative activity, and service work completed by Sue. This documentation supplied clear and undisputable facts, which provided the groundwork for an effective conversation.

Roberta went further by consulting with the previous department chair, Mike, about Sue's situation. Mike had been a mentor to Roberta and had encouraged her to apply for and accept the department chair appointment. Mike was trustworthy and not prone to gossip. It was during this conversation that Roberta learned of Sue's poor reputation when it came to service work. During the time when Mike was department chair, he received many complaints about Sue's lack of follow-through. Mike encouraged these colleagues who were complaining to have a conversation directly with Sue. Since that never happened, Sue's behavior continued unchecked.

Finally, Roberta consulted a long-time mentor, whose advice formed the basis of our next chapter, "Clarifying the Message." We will continue with Roberta and Sue's interaction and their effective difficult conversation as we proceed through each chapter.

ACTIVITY

Write down answers to the following questions about the difficult conversation you are facing.

- What documentation might be relevant to this conversation?
- What other people might be productively consulted before having this conversation?
- What personal information about you or the other person might be productive to consider in preparing for this conversation?

CHAPTER FOUR

Clarifying the Message

T HE LAST STEP OF PREPARATION IS TO CLARIFY YOUR MESSAGE. Every productive difficult conversation is guided by a clear message that you need the other person to hear and understand. Of course, as you will learn in the next chapter, many things will be said and heard during the conversation, but your task is to keep attention focused on the primary message that you need this person to hear and understand. In this chapter we will help you articulate a clear, succinct, direct, and compassionate message that you can use to guide a difficult conversation.

FACTS AND EXPECTATIONS

The first question that you need to ask yourself is, "What do I need to make sure is clear to this person?" No matter what else happens during this conversation, what do you need this person to understand when the conversation is over? We recommend focusing on the facts of the situation and the expectations you have for your colleague's performance. For example, perhaps you are dealing with a staff member who appears to have a chronic problem with punctuality. Following the previous steps, you have clear documentation about how often and when the person has been late to work. And you have a clear idea of what you expect of them; you expect them to arrive at work on time. Now, a moment to probe your expectations here might be in order. Are you expecting them to be in the parking lot on time? In the building on time? Or are you expecting them to be at their station and ready to work when their shift begins? These are the kinds of questions that you need to work through in order to arrive at a sufficiently clear message, one that would support a productive difficult conversation.

We recommend that the issues that you choose to handle in a single difficult conversation be kept to a minimum. This is not the time to attempt to handle every single infraction of every single rule of which you have made note. Almost no one can attempt meaningful behavior change when overwhelmed by too many behaviors to change or too many examples of when the behavior was performed inadequately. You and your employee will have a much more productive conversation and relationship if you are able to clearly target two to three specific behaviors that need to be changed.

Once you have begun to get clear on the facts of the situation and your expectations, it is time to write them down. And we mean for you to take this recommendation quite literally. We invite you to pull out a 3×5-inch card and write down the bullet points of your message. No dissertations. No wordy rationales and explanations. We recommend composing three to four bullet points, using words that you would actually voice in the conversation. If they won't fit on a 3×5 card, we invite you to consider that you might not yet be ready for the conversation. Too many issues, too many words, or lack of consideration of the specific words that you might use can lead to a conversation that gets off to a poor start, and sometimes recovery from a poor start can be difficult to accomplish.

As you compose your 3×5 card we recommend that you think of messages that are direct and compassionate. These are messages that state the facts clearly without attaching blame or shame. A direct message is one that is easy to comprehend even if it may be difficult to hear. For example, a difficult performance review conversation might begin with bullet points like these:

- Evaluations of your helpfulness at the reference desk have been lower than our target benchmarks for the last six months.

- The website project to which you have been assigned has been behind deadline for three months.
- We need to work together to get your evaluations up to the target benchmarks and help you meet deadlines.

Notice that these bullet points are not couched in polite language designed to ease the sting. Such polite language can often cloud the issues and leave the person unclear about the specific issues and concrete facts. Note also that these bullet points contain no language that implies fault or guilt. Such language can elicit defensiveness and then the conversation can turn into one about feelings rather than facts. Note finally that the final bullet point clearly points to the correction and uses the inclusive pronoun "we." This sets the table for a collaborative conversation about what each of you can do to correct the situation. It has been our experience that leaders who are willing to take on some of the responsibility for behavior change are leaders whose units consistently run more smoothly and whose morale is regularly healthier.

As you think about your 3 × 5-inch card statements, consider the options that you might be willing to use to help this employee respond more effectively to the expectations that you have. Perhaps you learn that this person is not someone who functions well in the mornings and something as simple as moving her to an afternoon shift would allow her to be more pleasant and attentive to library patrons. Or perhaps the challenges of the website project have outpaced her technical capacities and allowing her to attend some additional training would help her feel empowered to complete the project effectively and on time. Going into the conversation with an idea of the options that you would be willing to put into place to help the employee better meet expectations can greatly facilitate not only a productive difficult conversation but a more productive employee as well.

FILTER EMOTIONS

A final step in clarifying your message is once again a reflective one. Here we invite you to review your 3 × 5 card statements and make sure that they are written in a way that will help you speak them without any personal resentments or judgments that you might have built up. Resentments and judgments about the people we work with are natural; we all have them. If you are working closely with other people, you will eventually find yourself face-to-face with someone whose behavior gets on your nerves or worse, offends you. Trust us, you will not be able to have a productive difficult conversation unless and until you have fully reflected on these resentments and judgments and found a way to put them off to the side for the duration of the conversation.

For example, imagine that the person with whom you have to have the difficult conversation is someone who blows their nose *loudly* in front of patrons and coworkers all day long. This can be very irritating and it is certainly a behavior that you might need to address. You might have a desire to say something like "That behavior is rude and uncivilized, it has to stop." It is unlikely that you will be successful in addressing this behavior if you do so in the full flower of your irritation. Wait until you are not feeling especially irritated.

Or imagine that the person with whom you have to have a difficult conversation is someone who violates your personal work ethic. Maybe you believe that people should always be at work early and they should constantly be looking for new projects to enhance the productivity of the department. Perhaps the individuals with whom you must have this difficult conversation are a bit less committed than you; maybe they are always exactly on time to work but never early. Maybe they meet the minimal expectations of their assignments. Maybe this bothers and offends you deeply. Perhaps you are tempted to say something like, "I can't believe how little pride you take in your work. Aren't you embarrassed?" Unless these work ethic issues are germane to the issues sketched out on your 3 × 5 card, they have no place in your difficult conversation and you are ill-advised to proceed until you can make peace with the fact that the two of you approach work very differently.

Let's consider this step in light of the second difficult conversation that Roberta had to have with Sue. Recall from the last chapter that Roberta was a new department chair who failed, miserably by our standards, her first post-tenure review conversation with Sue. Five years later, during her second post-tenure review conversation with Sue, Roberta had learned and followed all the preparation steps we have advocated, including the creation of a 3 × 5 card. When she went into this second post-tenure review Roberta had a 3 × 5 card in her pocket with the following three bullet points:

- Student evaluations of Sue's teaching were below the standards deemed acceptable by the library
- No publications over the past twenty years

- None of Sue's colleagues wanted her on a committee because it was widely known that Sue would not follow through on assignments

Needless to say, this second post-tenure review conversation was far more effective because now both Roberta and Sue had a clear idea of the behaviors that needed to change.

A final note is in order. These first three chapters may evoke some anxiety; at first glance, the preparation that we advocate may seem to be quite time-consuming. You may wonder if you will have the time to prepare for the difficult conversations that you may face. In our experience, preparation takes much longer in the earlier stages of your supervisory experience. With time, you gain some instincts about what kind of information you need to hold on to and will learn how to move through some of these steps quite quickly.

ACTIVITY

Write down answers to the following prompts:

- What do you need to make sure is clear to this person?
    - » Facts of the situation
    - » Your expectations of them
- Write down your emotions and what you would like to say that would be unproductive to say.
- Now write down on a 3×5 card the facts of the situation and your expectations. Describe what you are willing to do to help this person succeed.

CHAPTER FIVE

During the Conversation

N THIS CHAPTER WE FOCUS ON THE HEART OF THE CONVER- sation. Now that we have sufficiently prepared for the conversation, it is equally important to consider what you will say during the conversation and, even more importantly, when and how you will respond to what the other person says.

We break this down into six parts, and discuss each in turn below. First, it is necessary to "State the Facts." It is important to begin the conversation well: starting off on the wrong foot could make a potentially constructive conversation go horribly wrong quickly. Stating the facts sounds simple, but there are both tricks to use and traps to avoid. Second, it is important to "Ask." You will see below that there are effective ways to ask questions and solicit information that yield positive results, and there are ways to ask things that can be both off-putting and combative. We offer ways to do the former and avoid the latter.

Third, it is most important to "Listen." Listening is easier for some than others. And not talking is hard for a lot of people. But this step is very important, and we spend time on it because it can be harder than it sounds. And then we talk about the fourth and equally important part, "Engage to Understand." This is a form of listening that allows for some talking. Therefore, it is trickier to balance, but we give you guidelines on how to do it effectively.

The fifth and sixth parts of this chapter deal with how to bring a difficult conversation to a close, outline how you will work together, and outline next steps along with detailing special aspects to notice during a conversation. These parts are labeled "Pay Attention" and "Explore Options," respectively. Taken together, it is our hope that this guidance will help bring about the result of a positive and successful though difficult conversation.

In addition, we highly recommend having these kinds of conversations in person rather than sending what you want to say over e-mail or in a letter. Once a person receives such an e-mail or letter, they are very likely to show up at your office wanting an explanation and you will need to have the difficult conversation anyway, only now it will be even more fraught with frustration from the employee.

STATE THE FACTS

As we discussed in chapters 2, 3, and 4, clarity and preparedness are the keys to beginning a successful conversation. It is important to state facts as simply and directly as possible at the beginning of the conversation, and you recall from chapter 4 that the 3×5-inch card exercise helps you get focused on the specific facts of the situation. To see how to do this, consider the following examples of work behavior that you may need to address.

One example: You supervise Jim, a generally good employee who has a habit of missing deadlines when assigned various tasks. This has been a pattern over several months and you want this behavior to stop. Another example: you supervise Jane, an employee that you perceive has a generally negative and obstructive attitude at work. This is fine until that negativity starts affecting the smooth running of meetings and deters other employees from sharing their ideas. A third example: Joy, a librarian you supervise, has started missing her shift assignments at a service desk and failed to show up to teach a class that was previously scheduled. This is new behavior, and you need to address it.

Since clarity and directness are important to a successful conversation, you must first begin by stating the facts. This is where your 3×5 card preparation comes in very handy. As often as possible, personally observe the behavior you want to change. The reason it is important to observe and make note of another person's behavior is that it allows you simply to state the facts of what you observed as a way to begin a difficult conversation. You won't be guessing at the person's motives or wondering about a person's personal struggles at home. You will just simply be observing.

Let's take the example of Joy who has started missing her shift assignments at a service desk and failed to show up to teach a class that was previously scheduled. You, her supervisor, have noticed this new behavior and you want to have a conversation about it. You could begin the conversation in the following way: "Thanks for making time to meet with me, Joy. I want to talk with you about a couple of times in the past week when I noticed you missed your service desk shifts and another time when you weren't around to teach a class that you had arranged. You missed your Monday and Thursday shifts, and on Tuesday a faculty member came to the library with their group of students expecting you to be available to teach a class."

You can have a similar conversation with the employee Jim, who misses project deadlines: "Jim, I have noticed that you have missed several project deadlines over the last several months. Two months ago, the Widget report was due on April 11, and you didn't turn it in until April 30. One month ago, I asked all employees to turn in budget reports by May 1, and you turned yours in a week late. And each Monday morning, I ask all employees to report on the number of hours they worked each week on a certain project. You have turned in this report late 5 out of the last 10 weeks."

Or take the example of Jane, the employee who is often negative at work and especially during staff meetings. Again, it is important just to state the facts: "Jane, during yesterday's meeting I noticed that you responded to suggestions made by your coworkers by saying either 'That's just stupid' or 'That's not going to help at all, so don't waste our time,' or phrases to that effect. I noticed this at least three times during that one meeting." Notice here that you do not say, "I noticed you were being negative," because that is an ambiguous fact at best. Instead, you need to state the facts as simply and objectively as possible without editorial slant or bias.

Let's return to our example of Roberta, the department chair, and Sue, her direct report who had a poor post-tenure review. Stating the facts looks almost identical to the 3 × 5 card and would sound something like this: "Sue, I hope you have had time to review the report from the ad hoc post-tenure review committee and the minutes from the meeting. Those documents identify three areas of concern: (1) teaching evaluations that have dropped below the department norm, (2) a dormant publication record, and (3) negative reports on your service records. Let's talk about each of these three concerns and identify a plan that will help you meet departmental expectations by the time of your next post-tenure review."

That's it. Just state the facts. We think you will find that starting difficult conversations by just stating the facts will make these types of conversations less difficult. Stating the facts also helps you avoid three typical pitfalls: (1) using "always" and "never"; (2) imputing motive to the person whose behavior you want to change, that is, thinking you know why they are doing what they are doing; and (3) using the phrase, "it has come to my attention," as opposed to being a firsthand witness to the behavior under discussion. Each of these pitfalls can send a difficult conversation off the rails.

1 Avoid using either of the words "Always" and "Never."

In the example of Joy missing her service desk shift, her supervisor might be tempted to say, "Joy, you are *always* missing your service desk shifts!" Or, in another situation involving the employee who is often late with reports, the supervisor might say, "You *never* turn in your reports on time." In dealing with the employee with a general negative attitude, the supervisor might be tempted to start by saying, "You're *always* negative." People often do this without thinking, mostly because they are frustrated with the behavior they have been observing. Each of these examples might lead the listener to become irritated and defensive. Each listener could immediately respond by saying, for example, "I was at the desk on time on Friday. I'm sorry you didn't notice that." Or, "I turn in most of my reports on time." And the listener could even say, "I'm not negative; I'm just voicing my opinion." Each of these responses can immediately derail the conversation. Therefore, by stating the facts simply and clearly, you avoid using the extreme words "always" and "never." "Always" and "never" are words that rarely apply to human beings who are frequently somewhere in-between.

2 Avoid imputing motive to the listener and her behavior.

In an effort to counteract our nervous feelings about having a difficult conversation, we are sometimes inclined to assume we know what the other individual is going through. The temptation is to state the facts, but also to include a statement about your own belief as to why the listener is doing what she is doing. For example, you might be tempted to begin the conversation with a statement like, "I know you're working hard." Or, after stating the facts, you might want to conclude by saying, "I know you're really overwhelmed right now," or "I know you're going through a hard time." These statements, although seemingly innocuous or even empathetic, could have the opposite effect: again, they could make the listener either defensive or irritated, and allow them to switch the topic of the conversation from the behavior that needs changing to whether the person is actually going through a hard time. In the end, the only person who knows what is going on with us is ourselves. Making any kind of statement about someone else's reasons for doing what they are doing is a distraction from the issue at hand.

3 As much as possible, avoid using the phrase, "It has come to my attention . . ."

Though very tempting, we encourage you not to use the phrase "It has come to my attention" or to say "I was told by someone that . . ." Generally speaking, try not to act on reports given to you by others. Sometimes you may have to, and we will discuss those situations below. As a rule, though, if you have prepared properly and have made notes of the incidents about which you want to talk, you should not have to say anything other than "I noticed" or "I saw."

When an employee comes to your office and says, "Joy missed her shifts at the service desk two times last week! You should do something about it!" you might be tempted to call Joy into your office and start the conversation with the phrase, "It has come to my attention." Usually, starting with this phrase leads Joy to realize that other people (her own colleagues!) have been talking about her behind her back and that these colleagues chose to come to you rather than talk to Joy directly. All of a sudden, the conversation is no longer about Joy's behavior, but rather about Joy asking you, "Who is talking about me? Why didn't they just talk to me about it?" Usually the conversation goes downhill from there. So when another employee comes to you with an observation about a fellow employee, it is better that you take the time to observe the behavior yourself. When told about Joy's absenteeism, make time to be near the service desk at the start of Joy's shift so you can observe the behavior yourself. And if it is a general complaint about an employee "always" being negative during meetings, make time to attend the meeting yourself so you can make the observation firsthand. Observing the behavior directly and speaking only on the basis of what you have observed avoid the pitfall of using the phrase, "It has come to my attention . . ."

Unfortunately, despite the best plans, sometimes you hear something about another employee that you cannot ignore and you cannot easily observe yourself. For example, imagine that an employee comes to you, their supervisor, to report that their coworker John was at a meeting in which he started yelling obscenities and slammed his fist on the table. If true, this is unacceptable behavior on John's part and a potential case of workplace violence. We say "if true" because you were not in attendance to witness John's behavior in person. As a supervisor, you need to address this behavior immediately, and there is no opportunity to attend future meetings. Even if you did, John may never repeat this behavior in front of you. Therefore, to have this difficult conversation we recommend starting the conversation with John by acknowledging that what you are going to talk with him about is hearsay, that you generally don't believe gossip, and that you are interested in what happened from his point of view. The conversation could start like this: "Thanks for taking some time to meet with me, John. I want to talk with you about the meeting you attended yesterday. Generally, I don't follow up on hearsay because it may not be true; however, this is too important for me to ignore. Knowing that hearsay may not be true, I'm very interested in hearing from you about what happened at the meeting."

We recommend using this technique to address those situations when you can't start the conversation with the preferred phrase, "I noticed . . ."

ASK

If the first thing you do during a difficult conversation is to "State the Facts" as described above, the next thing is to "Ask." Immediately following the stated facts, invite the other person to talk to you about their perspective or their point of view. Questions like the ones below will help the other person talk about the situation.

- "So, tell me what you think about this."
- "Tell me more about this from your perspective."
- "I want to understand your position, so tell me about your point of view."
- "Could you tell me about what happened?"

Let's consider how these "asking" phrases move the conversation from the "Statement of Facts" to the next step, "Listening." These "asking" phrases serve as a useful and necessary bridge to move a difficult conversation along.

Thus, in the case of Joy who has started missing her service desk shifts, you would first state the facts, "I noticed you missed your shifts on two different occasions," and then *ask,* "Could you tell me about what happened?" In the case of Jim, the employee who has missed several report deadlines, you could ask the same question. In the situation involving Jane, the negative employee who seems to badmouth ideas at meetings, you could try asking, "Tell me more about this from your perspective," or "I want to understand your position, so tell me about your point of view."

In the case of John, the employee who slammed his fist down on the table and shouted obscenities during a meeting that you did not attend yourself, notice that asking a question is almost inevitable since you did not witness the behavior. Therefore, stating the facts only as they were reported to you ("I want to talk with you about the meeting you attended yesterday"), you would move on to ask, "Knowing that hearsay is usually not true, I'm very interested in hearing from you about what happened at the meeting."

In the example of Roberta and Sue, in the second post-tenure review Roberta asked, "Your responses to these concerns are an important part of the post-tenure review process . What do you want the department and university to know about these three areas of concern?"

When you ask questions of those you supervise, do your best to make these actual questions without judgment, rather than statements disguised as questions. Statements like "Help me understand how you could possibly miss two service desk shifts last week," or "How could it be so hard to turn in your reports on time?" are really statements and not true questions. They will come across in a judgmental manner, which closes down the conversation. You want to avoid doing this as much as possible. Finally, bring your most curious self to the conversation. Being curious rather than immediately judgmental can make all the difference.

People are fascinating! Allow yourself to be curious about what drives this other person: how do they see themselves in the world, how do they view their work, and how do they rank priorities in their lives? The more we learn about others, the more we also learn about ourselves. Sometimes we learn about how different we are from other people, but more often we learn how much we are similar and this allows for compassion.

LISTEN

After you have stated the facts, and then asked the question, it is time to stop talking and listen. This will prove easier for some than others. However, it is essential that you find a way to listen, which means, *don't talk*. Let the person with whom you are having a difficult conversation do the talking.

In our opinion, this is the best part. It's the best part for four reasons: (1) listening opens a window into the mental process of another person; (2) listening might allow you to learn something new and important about your supervision; (3) listening allows us to demonstrate the most compassion; and (4) we don't have to do anything but listen. We discuss each of these in turn below.

1 Listening opens a window into the mental process of another person.

When we listen, we often hear something that is useful to the conversation. To illustrate this, we would like to expand on one of the examples we have used throughout this chapter involving Joy, the employee who has recently begun missing her shift assignments on a service desk in the library and has missed a class she was supposed to teach. This example of Joy is based on one of the author's real-life experiences she had with an employee. Below is a more complete presentation of the situation, which we provide here in order to illustrate not only the previously discussed principles of "stating the facts" and "asking," but also the most important step of "listening." Joy's name and some of the particulars have been changed to protect her identity.

Joy was a librarian still early in her career who missed two reference desk shifts entirely and who didn't show up for a class she had agreed to teach. Joy was a highly productive and reliable librarian who had never missed shifts or classes before. Her colleagues were noticing these omissions and brought the situation to the attention of the supervisor for the unit. To complicate matters further, Joy was up for promotion and tenure in six months. The process for promotion and tenure included letters from the other librarians and staff commenting on Joy's performance. Now that her colleagues had covered for her unexpectedly three different times in close succession, Joy's bid for promotion and tenure was at risk. A difficult conversation hosted by Joy's supervisor was required. Later, Joy told the supervisor that she knew what the conversation was about and that she was angry walking into the supervisor's office. The conversation went as follows.

Supervisor: Thanks for coming to meet with me, Joy. Normally, I wouldn't follow up on hearsay, but this is too important for me to ignore and I really want to understand what happened from your point of view. I understand that you missed two reference desk shifts last week and you didn't show up for a class you were supposed to teach. You are a very productive librarian and this isn't at all what I've come to know about you and your work, so I'm quite concerned about you. Can you tell me what happened?

Joy: I am under a lot of stress right now. I'm trying to move my mom into an assisted living home, my in-laws are in town for a visit, and we are moving in a month. I just got my calendar confused a few times. I was on my way to a meeting off campus when I realized I was supposed to be on the reference desk to work my scheduled shift. As for missing the class I was supposed to teach—I don't know what happened there. I must have forgotten to put it on my calendar [Joy was teary-eyed by this point.]

Supervisor: Wow, that is a lot. Life is stressful and yours sounds especially stressful right now.

By simply listening and giving Joy a chance to talk, it was obvious that her anger was quickly fading. By not trying to solve her personal problems or pass judgment on her life, Joy was no longer defensive. Moreover, it gave the supervisor a chance to evaluate the situation and begin to contemplate potential solutions. Of course, the conversation still needed to continue in regard to changing this behavior; what comes after the "listening" part of the difficult conversation is discussed in more detail below.

Even with great preparation and discipline, sometimes the listening portion of the conversation is very difficult. In the situation between Roberta and Sue, by the time the second post-tenure review came around, the feelings of resentment and doubt by department members had mounted and, honestly, Roberta's sympathies had waned. In the listening portion Sue engaged in a long and wandering explanation about why her publication record had been dormant. Roberta was about to stop listening but instead she redirected Sue to talk about the teaching and service concerns. Here she learned that Sue was deeply and genuinely shocked that her teaching evaluations were below the department norm and that her colleagues considered her an unreliable collaborator. This information allowed Roberta to reflect on all the ways in which Sue had become disengaged from the vitality of the department and to consider ways to help her become reengaged.

2 **Listening might allow you to learn something new and important about your supervision.**

It is impossible to know how our supervisory habits are experienced by others. Sometimes the only way to learn that something we are doing isn't working is by participating in a difficult conversation. One supervisor that we have worked with is a self-declared "southern woman." Which means that she appreciated the art of indirect communication, especially when it comes to assigning tasks. It has been much more comfortable for her to *ask* people to complete tasks rather than telling them to do so. When she observed that one of her employees wasn't following through on assigned tasks, she scheduled a difficult conversation. During the listening phase of this difficult conversation she learned that this employee took her "ask" quite literally. The employee said, "But you *asked* me to do that and so I didn't think it was required. I ran out of time and was focused on other tasks so I didn't think it was a big deal. I thought you were asking me to complete something if I had time." Unsurprisingly, this new supervisor quickly learned some more direct communication patterns.

3 **Listening allows us to demonstrate the most compassion.**

People with whom you need to have difficult conversations will likely be stressed, upset, worried, angry, confused, or in physical pain. Just because you might not be feeling any of these things when you start the difficult conversation and, even if you might deal with your feelings differently, the discomfort the other person might be feeling is no less real to them. Thus, while in the "listening" stage of the conversation we can empathize with the other person's discomfort and recognize that it is painful for them. Just being heard can be a healing moment for many people, and we as supervisors are in an excellent position to provide that moment. At the very least, we can be fascinated with the way people handle their lives.

4 **We don't have to do anything but listen.**

We don't have to solve anything, fix anything, or respond to anything. In fact, it is best if we simply make a mental note of what the other person is saying. Writing while another person is talking can be distracting.

However, while listening to the other person it is quite possible that the other person will start criticizing you and how you do your job. In other words, the above real-life conversation with Joy could have gone quite differently: after asking her to tell you what happened, she could have responded by launching into a tirade against you and the way you schedule the shifts on the service desk. She might have said something like, "I'm under a lot of stress right now. I would have come and talked to you about it, but you are never around. And even if I had, you probably would have said that no accommodations could be made for me. You don't really understand and appreciate what staff and librarians go through. So I missed a couple of shifts. Sorry." (This last would be said sarcastically.)

This type of outburst is replete with veiled and not so veiled criticism. When someone is critical of you, the temptation is to get defensive and respond, sometimes with your own anger. Since you are in the "listening" stage of the conversation, it is important to resist the temptation to get defensive. One trick you might use to resist the temptation to respond angrily is by writing down a few key words. Writing down a few key words also takes the sting out of the criticism and gives you a chance to consider the feedback more objectively and take a breath before responding.

This alternate version of the conversation with Joy demonstrates that in many instances the person with whom you are having a difficult conversation might be very upset. Some people demonstrate that upset in the form of tears and others in the form of outrage, interruptions, and accusations. If the conversation appears to be stalled either because you are now upset by the accusations or if the other person is just too upset to continue, consider ending the meeting. Ending a meeting under these circumstances can go something like this: "This conversation is becoming unproductive. Let's stop now, while we're ahead, and find some time tomorrow or the next day to continue. I know I need some time to think so that I can reenter the conversation in a more productive way."

We recommend that you refrain from suggesting that the other person needs to calm down. Telling another person to calm down can be an irritant to an already upset person, and can cause their emotions to escalate. Instead, as the example above illustrates, suggest to them that both you and they need time to think, which is likely to be true. This makes the exit strategy easier.

Finally, in yet other cases, the exact opposite might happen: after stating the facts and then asking the other person to describe what happened from their point of view, the other person could remain silent. We encourage you to allow the silence to last a little while, and then ask the person to voice what they are thinking. You could say something like: "It's difficult to interpret silence. Can you do any of your thinking out loud?"

If they are still silent, you have a couple of options to consider: you can move to exploring options for success (see more about this in the section below called "Exploring Options"); or you can give the person some time to think and come back for another meeting.

ENGAGE TO UNDERSTAND

In this section, we will review several tools that will assist with the skill of what we call "engage to understand." For those who have had some prior training or experience with management, engaging to understand will seem similar to the concept of "active listening." Lots of self-help books and training groups talk about "active listening." "Active listening" can be defined as "the act of mindfully hearing and attempting to comprehend the meaning of words spoken by another in a conversation or speech. Active listening is an important business communication skill, and it can involve making sounds that indicate attentiveness, as well as the listener giving feedback in the form of a paraphrased rendition of what has been said by the other party for their confirmation." ("Active Listening" 2016)

Our version of "active listening," by contrast, involves using our bodies and many of our senses to engage the other person in order to improve understanding. People who are listening to engage lean forward, use direct eye contact, and utilize nonverbal behaviors to indicate understanding, empathy, or when relevant, confusion. The reason we label this section "engage to understand" is because simply reflecting back to the other person what they said during a conversation is not always useful in all situations. With a better understanding of what another person is trying to convey, it is more likely that you will be able to have a more successful conversation and achieve the end result you desire.

One method for addressing criticisms is to get interested in what the other person is trying to say. Some of the ideas for engaging to understand comes from the book *Thanks for the Feedback: The Science and Art of Receiving Feedback Well,* in which the authors Douglas Stone and Sheila Heen (2014) provide a particularly useful recommendation that encourages us to "move from saying 'that's wrong' to 'tell me more'" as an effective way to respond to negative feedback (46). Asking another person to "tell me more" is not an admission that the other person is right. It is just a mechanism to increase understanding so that we can evaluate the feedback (47).

There are a couple of examples from real-life situations in which using the phrase "Tell me more" as part of engaging to understand is useful and helps makes difficult conversations less difficult. For example, in reorganizing a division of forty staff members, library administration had planned a number of meetings to invite feedback and to listen carefully to what was being said. At a later date, an employee stated, "Senior Administration is not listening to the concerns of those on the front lines." Since that statement seemed incongruent based on the number of meetings held inviting and listening to feedback, the comment was initially dismissed entirely. Fortunately, a colleague invited library administration to follow the advice of Stone and Heen (2014) above, namely, to ask this employee to "tell me more" (46). This colleague held another meeting to ask this employee and others in his unit to explain their point of view in more detail. This conversation brought out details that led to a much better understanding of what was behind that statement, and the change process was adjusted as a result.

Other portions of this same conversation led library administration to speculate that some employees were confusing "being listened to" with "being agreed with." In other words, it seemed that some employees believed that if library administration did not *agree* with them and implement their ideas, library administration was not *listening* to them. The truth of the matter was that library administration *had heard* their concerns, but simply disagreed that the concerns were enough to stop the reorganization. As Stone and Heen (2014) point out in their book, "Sometimes feedback that we know is wrong really is wrong. And sometimes, it's just feedback in our blind spot" (20). Asking another person to tell us more allows us to get the details that could encourage us to adjust what we are doing. Or it could just confirm that the feedback is wrong. If we don't make the crucial request to "Tell me more," we will never know.

Another example of how to engage to understand concerns a difficult conversation a supervisor had with an employee involving another library reorganization. This reorganization involved the entire library and almost every employee was affected by the change. Prior, during, and after the reorganization, the supervisor and other library administrators had communicated over e-mail, held focus groups, open forums, town halls, and all staff meetings; they conducted surveys and developed strategic directions and timelines. About eight months after the reorganization one of these supervisors held a regular meeting with an employee, in which the employee emphatically stated, "I don't know what's going on!" Again, the broad statement seemed incongruent with the amount of communication that had taken place. When asked to say more, the employee provided additional information:

- I don't know what is going to happen next.
- I'm confused about a particular decision that was made and the timing of the announcement.
- I understand what is going on but I just don't like it.

The first and third items were a reflection of the employee's anxiety and dislike of change. However, the second piece, "I'm confused about a particular decision that was made and the timing of the announcement," was a concrete request for additional information. This conversation more than any others was incredibly convincing that encouraging someone to "tell me more" (Stone and Heen, 46) could help one better understand what the other person was saying while remaining calm enough to evaluate the feedback. Was the feedback really wrong or was it feedback in a blind spot? (Stone and Heen, 20) We won't know unless we ask.

Finally, "tell me more" can be exceptionally useful when working with people who do a lot of thinking in their heads, but only give voice to the end result of that thinking. For example, an employee who is very smart and figures many things out in their head was working with her supervisor to make plans for a library event. When reviewing the action items, this employee blurted out, "What about Thursday?!" When presented with this seeming non sequitur, the obvious and gentle question comes to mind, "Could you tell me more about Thursday?" The employee had an excellent explanation in her mind and once she said all that she was thinking, her initial question made sense. There was indeed an issue with Thursday, which was easily straightened out.

Another tool to consider using in an effort to engage to understand is to repeat back what you heard. Each situation is different, so use this tool only as needed. The joy of using this tool is that the other person will immediately clarify if you get something wrong. As you repeat back what the other person has said, make sure your tone and words are nonjudgmental. If possible, be understanding of this person's plight if you are able. This tool is especially useful when working with people who are rambling or talking in circles and need help clarifying exactly what they mean.

Let's go back to the example of John in the meeting where he slammed his fist on the table.

Me: Thanks for taking some time to meet with me, John. I want to talk with you about the meeting you attended yesterday. Generally, I don't follow up on hearsay because it's usually not true; however, this is too important for me to ignore. Knowing that hearsay is usually not true, I'm very interested in hearing from you about what happened at the meeting.

John: I was upset because the group would not listen to me. The lack of open dialogue has created a strategic plan that seems to define something that is no longer a library at all. We used to value things like literacy, books, and reading, informed citizens, and the preservation of knowledge. If we allow food and drink into the library, it will destroy our ability to preserve the very items we collect and value. Allowing food and drink in the building will destroy our library values, and it sounds to me like the plan is to remove the library entirely and put something else in its place. For example, we brought together a committee to talk about what to remove from our collections before we had an opportunity to decide what we want in our print collection. Plus, if we allow food and drink into the building, how will that help with increasing circulation? I want an opportunity for the library to discuss our values before we go forward with making decisions. We need a collection policy that describes what we want in the collection and how we plan to preserve that, and preservation will ultimately mean no food and drink in the building. We frequently go down the wrong path because we haven't identified our values.

Me: Before you go on, let me see if I have this right. You were upset in a recent meeting because the group was discussing implementation of the strategic plan without having discussed what we value as a library. Part of implementing that strategic plan may allow for food and drink in the building. And it is your opinion that we need to discuss our values first. Is that right?

John: Yes!

Another recommendation from Stone and Heen (2014) that has made this portion of a difficult conversation just a little easier is "cultivating a growth identity" (183) or being in a learning state of mind. Even though you are justified in thinking you are a good communicator, for example, it is also true that you probably have more to learn and have improvements to make. Once you are able to expand your internal story to include learning, you will be much better able to respond to feedback that might otherwise be challenging to hear (194–95).

Incorporating these tools into difficult conversations should help you improve your understanding of what people are trying to say, even when what they are saying is cloaked in broad sweeping statements like "You're not listening to us," or "I don't know what's going on." Listening to understand is one of the most compassionate things we can do as human beings and is a critical component of having a difficult conversation.

PAY ATTENTION

Throughout the conversation we hope you will do everything in your power to devote your attention to just this conversation and only to the person with whom you are speaking. Managing attention is another critical communication behavior that can have a big impact on the outcome of any difficult conversation. We live in a world of constant disruptions and many of us have elevated multitasking to an art form; but in the world of important conversations, focused and dedicated attention is your strong ally. In this section we discuss how to begin the conversation, how to make sure you are able to attend only to this conversation, how to use nonverbal behaviors in a way to enhance a positive outcome, and how to manage the amount of time that you spend on this conversation.

Many of us have an instinct that any conversation needs a little "warming up." We've been socialized to begin conversations and meetings with a little small talk or catching up before we get to the business at hand. Recalling that every difficult conversation is unique and occurs in a specific context and relationship, we recommend as a general principle that this instinct for "warming up" is misplaced in the instance of difficult conversations. If both of you know that you have set aside some time to talk about a performance review or an issue of employment that needs some correction, spending time on small talk can be misleading and even disingenuous. And, because of this, engaging in small talk in these kinds of circumstances can have the opposite effect of warming up; it can actually enhance anxiety and stress. For this reason, we recommend getting to the point of the conversation pretty quickly. You might think about starting the meeting with a statement like, "Thank you for making the time to talk with me. I'm looking forward to learning what is happening for you and I think we can find a resolution that will support both of us."

Because difficult conversations can lead to difficult outcomes, we also advocate that you do everything that you can to limit the distractions that might compete for your attention during the conversation. Some of the simple things that you can do to limit distractions include the following:

- If you have an administrative assistant, ask them to attend to anyone who might be looking for you during the time that you have dedicated to this conversation.
- Ask that your calls be held for the duration of the conversation.
- Turn off any computer or phone alerts that might make distracting beeps and chirps during the conversation.

Visual elements of the space in which you will have this conversation can also be distracting. For many people, excessive clutter heightens anxiety. Excessive clutter can feel overwhelming and generate feelings about needing to escape. While we all know people who maintain and can operate quite effectively in an office space filled with piles of papers, files, and books, for many people, this kind of environment is not conducive to a positive outcome for a difficult conversation. For these reasons, we advise that you hold these conversations in a relatively clutter-free space. If you have a table in your office that can be easily made clutter-free, this might be an ideal space at which to hold this type of conversation. If not, perhaps there is a nearby conference room that can be used for a difficult conversation. Both of us are grateful to have tables

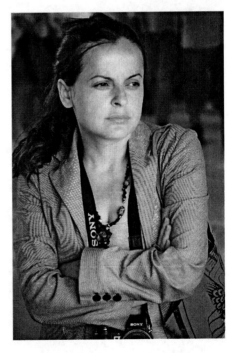

A series of non-immediate behaviors: scowling, arms crossed, lack of eye contact.
Photo by Joseph Kranak, CCBY

Immediacy cues on display: Gentleman on the left: open posture, smiling, eye contact. Gentleman on the right: leaning in, eye contact.
Photo by Liz West, CCBY

Immediacy cues on display: Leaning in, focused attention, eye contact, open postures.
Photo by Eugene Kim, CCBY

in our offices that we use for these types of conversations. Of course, privacy and quiet are essential so we advise that, in most cases, coffee shops and restaurants are not the best venues for conversations such as these.

As we've said throughout this book, difficult conversations are communication events, and as such communication concepts and research can be very helpful. Here we introduce you to a specific communication concept, "immediacy cues," with the promise that knowing about and using immediacy cues effectively can be quite powerful in just about any situation. In communication research immediacy cues are defined as "a cluster of nonverbal behaviors that function to reduce the psychological distance between a speaker and a hearer" (Anderson 1979). It is important to note that the definition begins with the phrase "a cluster." Single nonverbal behaviors hold little power to affect the outcome of an interaction, but a cluster of coherent behaviors can do much. Immediacy behaviors include open body positioning (i.e., no crossed arms or legs) that orients toward the hearer rather than facing away or off to the side. They also include appropriately extended eye contact. Eye contact can be a little tricky because norms about what is "appropriately extended" can differ from culture to culture. A general guideline is to look the other person directly in the eyes long enough to know that you and they have connected; let them be the first to divert their eyes. Movement is also an immediacy cue. Being overly still with an absence of gesturing is generally interpreted as non-immediate while leaning forward, nodding your head, and using some gestures are all behaviors associated with immediacy. Smiling is an immediacy behavior and, unsurprisingly, scowling is not. When used effectively and consistently, immediacy cues help to lessen any anxiety that might be associated with this conversation. In fact, classroom communication research demonstrates a very strong link between teachers trained to use immediacy cues and students who report liking the class, feeling motivated to learn, and recommending the class to others (Christophel 1990).

The real power of immediacy cues is that they are contagious. We humans tend to mirror each other unconsciously. We have an innate tendency to mimic the behaviors of those around us, especially those with whom we are close or who have influence over us. For example, when students smile and nod at their teachers their teachers tend to return those behaviors. This tendency toward mimicry is very important in the context of difficult conversations. Often we come to these conversations with some degree of anxiety, and the person with whom we are speaking can have even higher rates of anxiety. It is not uncommon for the other person to enter the conversation with crossed arms or legs (or both), a scowl, and averted eye contact. When that happens we are faced with a choice: we can let our body unconsciously mirror those non-immediate behaviors or we can assert some discipline and hold an open body position, direct eye contact, and a slight smile. If we can hold these immediate behaviors, no matter what the other person is doing, when we open the conversation it is very likely that the other person will begin mirroring our behaviors. When that happens, you can almost feel the anxiety lessening.

The last element of managing attention that is important to consider is time. As we have noted throughout this book, these difficult conversations are complex and emotionally intense. Managing the complexity and intensity requires a great deal of attention and energy, both of which are in limited supply, given that we are humans and are probably balancing a number of complex and intense issues. For this reason, we recommend that the time that you devote to these conversations be managed very carefully. In fact, we recommend that you dedicate no more than 20–30 minutes for these conversations. If you are very clear about the facts and your expectations (that is, you have completed your 3×5 card preparation before entering the conversation) and you listen carefully before going over some options for resolving the situation, you should not need more than 20–30 minutes. Staying within this time frame can help to keep the conversation focused on just the issues at hand, which is very important for a productive difficult conversation.

We know that sometimes difficult conversations seem to defy being held to this time frame. If the facts of the situation and your expectations for employee performance are not crystal clear in your mind, often these conversations get off to a poor start and much time is needed to clarify and recover. If you are not clear, it is impossible for the other person to develop a clear understanding about why you have asked to have this difficult conversation and what you want changed. Rather than extend the time of the conversation, we recommend ending the conversation at the appointed time and rescheduling so that you can better prepare a clear and direct message about the facts and your expectations.

Sometimes the other person reacts with excessive and time-consuming emotion. Sometimes this takes the form of tears, other times it takes the form of anger, and still other times it takes the form of loquacious explanations and excuses. We admit, these reactions are difficult if not impossible to control. And, it is important to note that you probably cannot get to a productive resolution until these emotional reactions have been spent. Sometimes the listening portion of the difficult conversation takes up most of the 20–30 minutes because of the emotion behind the person's reactions. We advise that you allow the person to emote, unless the anger becomes too violent for you to tolerate, and then close the conversation at the appointed time. A rescheduled appointment to focus on options for change will be much more productive than attempting to move forward with so many unresolved emotions.

We recommend using the phrase "I'm noticing the time . . ." or something similar as one way to bring a conversation to a close that has reached the thirty-minute time frame. For example, if you as the supervisor have arranged a thirty-minute meeting with an employee and the meeting has gone on for the full thirty minutes without resolution, you could say something like this: "I'm noticing the time and we are at the end of the time we scheduled for this meeting. Since we aren't finished talking, let's set up another time to finish this conversation."

A final word about anger. We all have different tolerances for expressed anger and it is important to know and respect your own. Aside from physical violence, which should never be tolerated under any circumstances, expressions of and responses to anger can have a great range. In the case of any physical violence, stop the conversation, get out of the space, and call security. Period. But in the case of other expressions of anger, responses can be quite individualized. Consider a few examples.

Andrea was an associate professor and a new department chair. A former chair, who was male and a full professor, was not entirely thrilled with her appointment. He was unhappy with a decision that she'd made and came to her office unannounced, stood over her desk, and began speaking in a loud voice. What would you do in this situation? There are many things you might do. You could tell him to get out of your office until he calmed down. You could tell him he needed to schedule an appointment. Or you could stand up, repeat your rationale for your decision, and tell him how to appeal the decision. Regardless of your chosen response, this conversation should not extend beyond twenty minutes.

Tom, an associate chair who was responsible for scheduling classes, made a decision not to rehire a part-time teacher whose course evaluations were quite poor. During the scheduled difficult conversation, the part-time teacher began screaming and pounding on the table. Again, there are a number of responses that might be used in this situation. You could terminate the conversation, call security, or listen empathically. Listening empathically, mirroring immediacy behaviors, might bring the conversation to a more stable level and allow you to proceed to a productive closure. Perhaps this colleague could benefit from some training that would help him become a more successful classroom teacher. If you can get to a calm conversational tone in less than 20–30 minutes, great! If not, reschedule once you've let the other person know that you feel their pain and look forward to discussing some reasonable options in your next conversation.

EXPLORE OPTIONS

Now that you've stated the facts and listened carefully, it's time to consider how the situation might be resolved to everyone's satisfaction. This resolution will emerge from the conversation, but our experience has taught us that it's wise to enter these conversations with some ideas about a resolution that you might be able to support. Sometimes these conversations can be sufficiently difficult that both of you lose sight of options that might create positive results for both of you. It can be very useful to be able to introduce some ideas that might be productive given that your conversational partner will also have some input. In the end, you want to find a resolution that works well for both of you; you want a resolution that will allow both of you to succeed.

When entering this phase of the conversation, it is important to emphasize that you want this person to succeed and that you want their help in finding a resolution that will work for both of you. This verbal confirmation that you are cheering for the person's success can take quite a bit of the sting out of a conversation that may have been about their lack of success.

Let's consider some examples. Many of you will encounter issues of punctuality. Getting to work on time can be so hard for some of us; in fact, this is such a common issue that we have used several such examples in this book. When going into a difficult conversation about punctuality, it can be good to consider if and how you might be able to adjust the employee's schedule so that punctuality can be more easily attained. Or consider an employee who seems to be procrastinating on a task that they've been assigned. When heading into this conversation you might consider whether or not the skills required to complete the task well exceed those the employee feels confident using. If, through the conversation, you learn that this is indeed the case, you might be prepared to fund some additional training so that the employee can enhance those skills. Of course there are always those behaviors that are less easily changed. Maybe the employee has a very loud voice and disturbs those around him with loud conversations and phone calls. In this instance it might be prudent to think about a different working station for the employee, maybe some place a little more isolated.

Let's go back to the conversation with Joy. Here is the conversation so far:

Supervisor: Thanks for coming to meet with me, Joy. Normally, I wouldn't follow up on hearsay, but this is too important for me to ignore and I really want to understand what happened from your point of view. I understand that you missed two reference desk shifts last week and you didn't show up for a class you were supposed to teach. You are a very productive librarian and this isn't at all what I've come to know about you and your work, so I'm quite concerned about you. Can you tell me what happened?

Joy: I am under a lot of stress right now. I'm trying to move my mom into an assisted living home, my in-laws are in town for a visit, and we are moving in a month. I just got my calendar confused a few times. I was on my way to a meeting off campus when I realized I was supposed to be on the reference desk to work my scheduled shift. As for missing the class I was supposed to teach—I don't know what happened there. I must have forgotten to put it on my calendar.

Supervisor: Wow, that is a lot. Life is stressful and yours sounds especially stressful right now.

Now the supervisor can move into problem-solving and exploring options.

Supervisor: I am concerned, though, that your bid for promotion and tenure is coming up in just six months and the colleagues who have covered for you are not at all pleased. And those will be the same people writing letters during your review. Let's talk about how to fix this.

Joy: I don't know what to do! I'm so overwhelmed.

Supervisor: You are an excellent librarian and I want you to have a successful bid for promotion and tenure. From now on, let's make your highest priority meeting your commitments to the reference desk and the classes you teach. If you are on your way to a meeting and realize you forgot about a desk shift, turn around and come back.

The conversation continued a short time longer with a few "what about if this happens" from Joy and the supervisor's consistent redirection of her back to her commitments. They left on good terms, with Joy thanking the supervisor for her concern for her. Joy took the direction, adjusted her priorities, and made a successful bid for promotion and tenure. It doesn't always work this way. Joy was, in fact, a very productive librarian. She just needed a bit more direction and a clear path to fixing the situation.

Whatever the solution, reaching it together can be a powerful motivator for the employee. Even better, there can be even more motivation if the employee can bring a solution to the problem that is acceptable to you.

In the example of Roberta and Sue, after Roberta learned how disconnected Sue had become from the vitality of the department, they worked to find ways to close that gap. On the issue of course evaluations, they agreed that Sue would review the course evaluations of her colleagues in order to get a more current view of the instructional norms in the department. Sue also worked with a research mentor of her choosing to help transform her most recent conference paper into a publication. And Roberta assigned a new service task to Sue, one that did not require much collaboration but that would allow her to begin to develop a positive service record. Roberta and Sue worked toward each of these agreements collaboratively.

ACTIVITY

Using the table below, either write down the requested information about a real conversation you had, or use a conversation that you will have to have at some point after reading this book, but have been putting off because it is a difficult conversation that you are dreading.

How the conversation went	What did not go as expected	What to do differently
▪ State the facts	▪ State the facts	▪ State the facts
▪ Ask	▪ Ask	▪ Ask
▪ Listen	▪ Listen	▪ Listen
▪ Engage to understand	▪ Engage to understand	▪ Engage to understand
▪ Explore options	▪ Explore options	▪ Explore options

CHAPTER SIX

You're Not Finished until You Write It Up

IN THIS CHAPTER, WE GIVE YOU THE TOOLS TO HOLD YOURSELF and others accountable. That is to say, we talk about how to make sure that the person with whom you spoke understands what needs to change, and by when you want them to change it. In addition, it is equally important that you keep track of anything that you have promised to do, or to make sure that you have the tools to follow through with any action on your part that you may have to take. It all comes down to documentation: without documentation, it will be as if the conversation never happened; and considering the amount of time you have already given this process, you want to make sure you have captured the conversation. This next step of writing down the conversation is crucial to a difficult conversation's ultimate success.

It is important to take time as soon as possible after the conversation with your employee to write up what happened, that is, record the conversation. Do it as soon as possible while your memory of the conversation is still fresh. If you did end up taking notes during the conversation, make sure to incorporate those into your description of the conversation. Since it is likely that you will be sending your notes over e-mail, writing the conversation up as a draft e-mail or a document you can later attach to an e-mail is useful.

Next, we discuss what to do should the employee respond negatively or not respond at all to the write-up of the conversation. As you will see below, when you write up the conversation, you will give the other person a chance to respond. In this chapter, we address the many ways you can write up a difficult conversation and we talk about how many times you need to go back and forth with the other person regarding the accuracy of a write-up. In the next chapter, we will talk about how to make an informal write-up more formal, if necessary, including how to move matters along to the next level.

Most importantly, no matter what the situation is, when you have had a difficult conversation you need to write it up. Even if the conversation did not go the way you may have wanted, you still need to write it up. You will see in several examples below that no matter the variety and outcome of difficult conversations, it is always in your best interest to write it up.

RECORD A CONVERSATION

When this is the first difficult conversation you have had with a particular employee regarding a specific behavior, the write-up will be different than if this is the third or fourth conversation about the same issues with the same employee. Each difficult conversation is different depending on whether it is addressing the same behavior or different behavior with the same employee. Generally speaking, if this is the first conversation about a certain issue, we recommend keeping the write-up as informal as possible by sending it as an e-mail to the other person. Should you eventually have to send it as a formal letter of reprimand in the future, you can easily convert it to a letter. Nevertheless, it is sufficient and recommended to send it as an informal e-mail initially. It should contain the following content:

1. Start by thanking them for meeting with you and including the date of the meeting.
2. Relay what was said during the conversation.
3. Include anything the employee agreed to do, including any changes in behavior.
4. Include anything you agreed to do.

5. Ask the other person to correct any misunderstandings, omissions, or misstatements that they believe are in the write-up.
6. Most importantly, clearly state a specific date by which you need to have a reply.
7. Finally, use the write-up to introduce forgotten or postponed issues, if applicable.

Let's take each piece individually using a variety of examples, but mostly focusing on the previous example of Joy, the librarian who missed two reference desk shifts and who didn't show up for a class she had agreed to teach.

1 Start by saying "Thank you."

Thanking the other person for their time and for meeting with you is a generous way to start the e-mail. In this beginning portion of the e-mail, we recommend giving a short reason for the meeting notes as a way to make this less threatening to the other person. Also, for potential future legal and disciplinary reasons, place the date you had the meeting in the subject line of your e-mail. You might want to write something like this:

> **Date:** Thursday, May 26, 2016 at 8:58 PM
> **To:** Joy Matthews <joy.matthews@college.edu>
> **Subject:** Meeting Notes for May 26
>
> Hi Joy,
> Thanks for taking the time to meet with me today. We talked about many things during our meeting, so I wanted to take a minute to capture what we discussed and our action items so that I can be sure we heard the same things.

2 Relay what was said during the conversation as completely and accurately as possible.

This is an opportunity to document what prompted the meeting in the first place and what you heard from the other person. Hopefully, if you followed our advice in chapter 5 on how to have a difficult conversation, this part of the write-up should consist of the same "statement of facts" that prompted the meeting, the "ask," and then the employee's reply, that is, what they said when you were "listening" and "engaging to understand." In writing up what the employee said in response to the "ask," it is not always necessary to write up everything the employee said, but it is important to get the gist of it. Each case will be different, and when in doubt, write more than less.

Using the example of Joy again, the write-up could go something like this:

> We began our conversation with me stating that I noticed you had missed two reference desk shifts and a class you were scheduled to teach. When I asked you to tell me what happened, you indicated that you were under a lot of stress these days because you were taking care of a number of personal issues. I put all of this recent activity in the context of your upcoming bid for promotion where your colleagues will be writing letters commenting on your performance. I pointed out that your colleagues covered for your unexpected absences and are probably not pleased. I told you that I sincerely want you to succeed in your bid for promotion and that I'm concerned about these absences interfering with that process.

Please note that it is probably not necessary to detail each of the three personal issues Joy conveyed: that she is dealing with moving her mother into a care facility, that she is moving herself, and that her in-laws are visiting. Briefly summarizing a long list of personal issues is completely appropriate. Similarly, as in the example of John, the employee who reportedly slammed his fist on the table during a meeting, you might get a ten-minute diatribe in response to your "ask." You cannot possibly write down everything the employee might say in such situations, but do your best to get the gist of it. Moreover, as we will discuss in more detail below, the employee will get their chance to let you know everything you may have missed in the write-up.

In cases in which you were unable to witness the employee's behavior personally, like with the example of John, who supposedly yelled obscenities and slammed his fist during a meeting you were not at, the e-mail write-up could go like this:

> We began our conversation with me stating that I normally don't like to act on rumors, but this issue was too important for me to ignore. I stated that it had come to my attention that you were at a meeting the other day in which you raised your voice, using what some would consider vulgar language, name calling, and slamming your fist on the table. I told you during our conversation that I don't like listening to

> secondhand accounts and rumors because they are often not true or highly exaggerated, but this involved potential workplace violence and so it was necessary to talk to you about it. I said that I was very interested in hearing what happened from your point of view. You responded by saying that you did not raise your voice, you do not remember using any vulgar language or calling anyone names, and that you may have tapped the table a couple of times to emphasize your point, but that it certainly wasn't slamming your fist.

This example illustrates two things: try to be complete in stating the facts that prompted the meeting in the first place; and faithfully write up what the employee said in response, even if it is a complete denial. Remember, the point of the write-up is faithfully to record what you and the employee said, and not to make any judgments or convey opinions that were not expressed. Thus, it would not be appropriate to insert editorial comments like, "Remarkably, you denied everything," or "John was agitated and upset throughout our conversation." Instead, describe John's behavior and remove your assumptions about what those behaviors might mean. For example, "John did not make eye contact, crossed his arms, and constantly clicked his pen throughout the conversation."

In addition, you need to write up the conversation no matter how it turns out. That includes conversations that stalled because either you or the other person got too upset to continue, and so you ended the conversation. In writing up such an abbreviated conversation, you would write:

> After I asked you to tell me what happened from your perspective, you began stating how unfair everything is, and that you felt persecuted. When you paused, I stated that I did not think it would be productive for us to continue the conversation. I said I would like to end this meeting, but that I would reschedule it for tomorrow or the next day so that we both have a chance to think.

Thus, no matter how the conversation goes, it is important to relay the conversation as completely and accurately as possible.

3 Include anything the employee agreed to do.

Writing down what the employee agreed to do is necessary to hold them accountable later. Continuing to use Joy as our example, here is what documenting her agreement would look like:

> We agreed that one way to fix this would be for you to adjust your priorities so that your commitments to the service desk and your classes would remain your top priorities. You agreed that should you be on your way to a meeting or a conference and suddenly remember that you have a commitment back at the library, that you would immediately turn around and come back.

Let's consider another example, this one involving an employee who is consistently missing due dates for assignments. In this example, the agreement to action items might consist of stating, "We agreed that you would meet all future deadlines as assigned." And if the situation was one in which an employee used name calling and fist pounding during a meeting, the agreement might consist of stating, "Even though you described the incident differently than what was reported to me, you agreed to not use language or words that most other people would find offensive, even though you yourself might not find them offensive. And you also agreed that under no circumstances will you ever strike your fist on a table, chair, wall, or door during meetings with fellow employees."

In cases in which the employee completely denies having done any of the things reported to you, the write-up needs to reflect this: "You said that none of the things reported actually occurred. I then pointed out that swearing, yelling, and slamming fists on tables would be unacceptable behavior according to the personnel policy manual had it occurred, and asked you if you understood that. You said yes, you understood, but again reiterated that you didn't do any of the things of which you were accused." Even though it may seem that you did not accomplish anything during this conversation, it is still important to write it up. You never know when it will be relevant to some future conversation.

4 Include anything you agreed to do.

We encourage you to be a role model for follow-through on what you agree to do. Your employees are taking their cues from you about timeliness and keeping commitments. Your ability to demonstrate that you are willing to do your part, and that you are able to keep your commitments, will do more to encourage the other person to hold up their end of the bargain than anything you might say. Continuing with the example of Joy, you would write:

> I agreed to set up meetings with you every other week to follow up on
> your progress and make sure that you were on track to make a successful
> bid for promotion.

In addition, in the case of needing to schedule a follow-up meeting, make
sure you do that too. Don't leave the employee hanging and wondering what
is coming next: make sure you keep up your end of the agreement.

5 Ask the other person to send corrections.

We recommend offering the other person an opportunity to send corrections to
your e-mail write-up. Even though you are probably certain you have recorded
the conversation accurately, you should not be surprised if the other person
has a completely different memory of what was said. Therefore, be prepared
to hear that you "got it all wrong." This part looks something like this:

> Would you take a look at these notes and let me know if I misunderstood
> anything and send me any corrections by Tuesday, May 31? Thanks for
> your help in making sure we are on the same page.

6 Specify a date by which you need a reply.

This is very important, especially in cases in which the other person does not
send any reply at all. Even though you have given the other person a chance
to make corrections to the e-mail write-up, you don't want that process to last
forever. Therefore, providing a due date for changes is a helpful mechanism.
When this is the first difficult conversation you have had with a particular
employee regarding a specific behavior, it is important to be informal about
the tone of the notes, so initially just asking for their review of the notes and
any corrections is sufficient, as we demonstrated above.

7 Introduce forgotten or postponed issues, if applicable.

Difficult conversations are challenging, and we are frequently nervous
having these conversations even when we are prepared. The authors have

had moments when they intended to cover three issues, and were only brave enough to bring up two. Alternatively, in assigning action items, we might forget to recommend a due date. The e-mail write-up can be a way to fix this. You could say something like, "One other thing I would like to discuss at our next meeting is your attendance at the conference in October." This will help keep you accountable to discuss this item at the next meeting. If the topic is too sensitive to bring up over e-mail, make a note to yourself to have the conversation the next time you meet with this person.

Due dates can also be assigned post-meeting: "During our conversation I forgot to give us due dates for our assignments. I'll get you the statistics you need by tomorrow, May 27, and then I'll need the report from you in two weeks, on Thursday, June 9. Let me know right away if that due date is not workable for you." If the due date is flexible, it is helpful to allow the other person a moment to negotiate. If the due date is not flexible, then end with, "I'll need the report from you in two weeks, on Thursday, June 9."

MANAGE THE UNEXPECTED RESPONSE

While there may be many responses to your meeting notes, two of the most typical are someone who does not reply and someone who indicates that you are completely mistaken in what happened during the meeting. It is important to remember that one of the reasons for writing up a difficult conversation is to start a paper trail that may be necessary if you need to take further steps with the employee or coworker. Thus, if the employee's problematic behavior continues, it may be necessary to be able to document previous conversations you had with her. Moreover, in the case of a coworker, if the behavior does not change and you need to go to your supervisor, you will be able to show them what attempts you have already made to resolve the issue. In any event, you might eventually need the write-up to respond to any claims by an employee or coworker that this is the first time they are hearing of this. The write-up and the structure for it we outlined above will prove useful if you need to take further steps. We discuss this possibility in more detail in the next chapter.

1 No Reply

When having a difficult conversation, and in writing it up when finished, we believe that it is best to assume good intentions and keep the tone of the meeting and the write-up friendly and informal. For purposes of the write-up, you can create a friendly and informal tone by simply relating the conversation without editorial comments. It is then best to conclude with a simple request for a response by a particular date. If the employee does not reply, you will probably have to schedule a follow-up meeting. For this follow-up meeting, you should print out the notes and ask the employee if she received them and if she has any questions about them. Whatever her response, you will need to clarify at that point that no response from her about the meeting notes, either now or in the future, is an indication of agreement with what was written. Again, keep this conversation informal and friendly:

> Since this is the first time I had to have this conversation with you, I want to make sure that you know if I don't hear back from you about meeting notes by the due date, I will assume you agree with the notes as I have written them. If you don't agree with them, that's ok, just say so. Your help with reviewing the meeting notes will keep us on the same page and make sure we limit misunderstandings between us.

You can also spell out in the meeting notes that if she does not respond, you assume that she is in agreement with the notes as written. Again, we recommend employing these measures only if the employee is not responding or insisting that she never received your e-mail. This concluding part of the meeting notes could go something like this:

> Would you take a look at these notes and let me know if this is a complete and accurate reflection of our conversation? Please send me any corrections by end of business Tuesday, May 31. If I don't hear from you by that date, I'll assume that you agree with what I wrote. Thanks for your help in making sure we are on the same page.

2 You got everything wrong!

Sometimes you will get something wrong. If the other person points out a legitimate incorrect statement or you got a date wrong or some other simple item, send a quick e-mail back acknowledging that the other person was right. Thank her for her response.

If, however, the other person goes into a long e-mail about how different the conversation went, send a short e-mail acknowledging your receipt of her e-mail and suggest that the two of you talk about it at a future meeting. It is rarely a good idea to write another long e-mail correcting the person's misunderstandings point by point. It is better to start over. In the next conversation, we recommend checking in with the other person more frequently to make sure you are both in agreement. For example:

You: Ok, I want to go over what we talked about and our action items. Let's start with what we talked about. You thought what I said last time was just a suggestion, not an actual thing you were supposed to do. Does that sound right?

Other Person: Yep, so far, so good.

You: All right, so I agreed that I would be more direct when I want you to do something and not disguise it as a suggestion or a question with options, but as a direction. You agreed to get clarification from me if you were ever confused. Does that sound about right?

Other Person: Well, no, I never agreed to get clarification from you.

You: Oh, my mistake. Please get clarification from me if you are ever confused. Can you agree to that?

You will notice that this second or possibly third conversation, if necessary, continues to follow the steps, "state the facts, ask, and then listen," but it is used more frequently so that each section of the conversation is as clear as possible, making the write-up afterwards a little easier and hopefully, something the other person agrees with. It is an important step in creating a paper trail that you might need in the worst case: officially disciplining the employee. Even though you started the conversation casually and with the best intentions of "engaging to understand," sometimes it may be necessary to move the process along to a more formal reprimand. The write-up will be a necessary step in that process. Remember: be positive and expect the best outcome possible, but be prepared to move things along to the next level if necessary.

Once you begin to have difficult conversations or if you are anticipating a difficult conversation, we recommend discussing the issue with your Human Resources person. They must keep most conversations confidential and are very likely to have good advice for you to consider prior to having a conversation. Conversations that Human Resources cannot keep confidential are any indication of sexual harassment and any indication that you or someone else is likely to do physical harm to someone. After the conversation, let Human Resources know how it went and continue to keep them in the loop periodically as you work through this process.

ACTIVITY

Write a draft follow-up e-mail message.

- Remember to include the facts of the situation, anything the employee agreed to do, and anything you agreed to do to help them succeed.
- Ask for their review and edits of the notes by a particular date.

CHAPTER SEVEN

Keep up the Good Work

IN THIS CHAPTER, WE ENCOURAGE YOU TO KEEP UP REGULAR meetings and continue to write up the results of those meetings. It is tempting after a difficult conversation to avoid the other person. We recommend conducting your business normally, look the other person in the eye, greet them the way you always have, and continue in good faith that all will be well. This quiet confidence and warm greeting serves the purpose of keeping you from holding resentments and gives the other person the opportunity to see that you are giving them a chance to turn things around.

One of the authors had the experience of not getting along well with her boss. There were frequent misunderstandings, the supervisor would panic about issues that were well under control, and the supervisor began to microman-age the work. The author began canceling her meetings with this supervisor and limiting her in-person communications with her. After one particularly distressing incident, the author went to a trusted advisor in the same unit and asked for advice in working with the supervisor. The advice given was to meet with the supervisor more often. This seemed entirely wrong! However, desperation made the advice more palatable. Sure enough, with regular and more frequent meetings the relationship with this supervisor improved dramatically. The more the supervisor felt in the loop, the more she was able to relax and step back.

This same advice is true when it comes to meeting with people with whom there are misunderstandings or behaviors we want to change. Even if we dread the conversations, it is still better to have meetings on a regular basis and scheduled in advance. Scheduling meetings in advance has the advantage of not needing to set a special meeting for a difficult conversation. Regular meetings also allow you to create consistent meeting notes as follow-up to each conversation. These notes will be useful in establishing a pattern of improvement or noncompliance. The notes make sure that the other person is not surprised during their performance evaluation when you refer to the issues you were working on together.

TALK TO HUMAN RESOURCES

It is in everyone's best interest that your employees are successful and it is best to provide them with as much opportunity for success as you are able. When an employee makes a decision not to comply with what you are asking them to do, the documentation you created will help you demonstrate this pattern. As mentioned in the last chapter, we encourage you to inform your Human Resources person of the conversations you plan to have with another person and to keep Human Resources in the loop periodically about how things are going. They will know your institution's employment rules and the employment laws of the state. For example, Human Resources can guide you about how much documentation is enough documentation before moving forward with disciplinary action. They can give parameters for what disciplinary action looks like, when you need to write up any documentation on official letterhead, what documentation goes into a personnel file, and how many official warnings need to take place before dismissal. They can provide advice on wording for documentation and warnings, and present other mechanisms for encouraging success. No matter where you work, your institution will likely have unique methods and requirements for personnel actions. Learning about these in advance will make it easier to move toward a conclusion should the employee choose not to comply with what you are asking them to do.

It is important to note that Human Resources representatives, like all employees, can sometimes disappoint us. One of the authors had the experience of receiving incomplete information about the disciplinary and dismissal processes, which almost derailed a year's worth of work with a noncompliant employee. Hopefully this experience is rare, and it in fact is isolated in our own experiences, but because of this experience, we recommend asking several Human Resources people their advice regarding what you need for disciplinary action and dismissal proceedings. Ask the Human Resources team within your library, if your library is large enough to have Human Resources personnel, and ask the Human Resources team located centrally for the institution. Continue to ask until you get some consistency and agreement about the process or until you find someone you are confident can guide you accurately through the process. It is likely that your institution will have at least some written policies about disciplinary action and dismissal proceedings for employees. Read this documentation thoroughly as you make plans for working with your Human Resources team. It is almost always better to have an abundance of information.

Another experience of one of the authors was working in a unionized environment. In these cases, documentation regarding the process for disciplinary action is usually very thorough, which can be helpful. Keep in mind that moving into disciplinary action will likely mean meetings that include the employee, their union representative, and a member of the Human Resources team.

No matter what procedures and policies your institution has, regular meetings with consistent meeting notes will be required to demonstrate how you have provided clear expectations, mechanisms for employee success, and documentation that demonstrates a pattern of noncompliance. Keeping up regular meetings with another person is an exceptionally useful way to hold them and yourself accountable. The documentation you create as a result will objectively tell the story of how you tried to encourage the employee to succeed and their decision not to comply with your reasonable requests, like "Don't miss your shifts," or "You need to get your reports in on time." This objectivity is mandatory if you want to see improvement or if you are forced to move forward with disciplinary actions.

THE END OF OUR STORIES

In the case of Joy, the librarian who missed two reference desk shifts and who did not show up for a class she had agreed to teach, the outcome was quite positive. She took our conversation very seriously and rearranged her priorities. Over the next six months leading to her bid for promotion, she met all of her commitments without unexpected absences. Her bid for promotion and tenure was successful and she has continued her career very effectively since then.

As for John, the employee who slammed his fist down on the table and shouted obscenities during a meeting, he initially consulted with a counselor through the Employee Assistance Program and this behavior did not appear again for some time. However, additional changes in organizational structure and his refusal to continue working with a counselor brought the behaviors back with even more force. Since John refused to admit needing additional help through the Employee Assistance Program, we had no choice but to follow through on a formal reprimand and move toward dismissal.

Jane, the employee who was often negative at work and especially during staff meetings, decided to retire early since she was unhappy about the direction in which the library was moving.

With Jim, who missed project deadlines but was otherwise a good employee, we made a number of agreements that brought him into better alignment with due dates. For example, he agreed that assigned due dates would actually be one week in advance of when they were due. (Sometimes setting your clock ahead ten minutes really does help you be on time.) During our meetings, we would discuss what steps needed to be taken next, and we would assign a due date to each one. Though never perfect, Jim began to meet more deadlines and his supervisor was clear about his progress toward those deadlines. Additionally, there was now an established way to discuss the issues when Jim was late with his reports.

After several more years of uneven performance, Sue was eventually put on annual post-tenure reviews and ultimately was forced to retire. This was a very complicated case, but we wonder how much time, anxiety, and attention might have been saved had Roberta been more prepared and self-reflective before that very first post-tenure review conversation.

CHAPTER EIGHT

Coworkers

EVEN IF YOU GET TO WORK WITH PEOPLE YOU GENUINELY LIKE, you are still likely to be in conflict with one of them at some point. On any level in the organization you may need to have a difficult conversation with a coworker who is doing something you would like them to stop doing, like interrupting you when you are trying to work; or asking them to do something they don't want to do, like closing their door when they engage in personal phone calls. In this chapter, we describe how to manage these tricky situations where you need a colleague to stop doing something they like to do or to do something they may not want to do.

Let's use the step-by-step instructions to manage several examples of difficult conversations with a colleague: (1) a coworker who occupies an open cubicle next to yours is on their cell phone four or five times a day, engaged in loud, personal conversations that are not work-related and are very distracting and unsettling; (2) an angry e-mail sent in response to your e-mail that was not intended to offend; and (3) a situation where you and a colleague are working together on a project and the colleague has missed an agreed-upon deadline.

GETTING CLEAR

The tricky thing about coworker situations is deciding whether this is a conversation you need to have or your boss needs to have. In each coworker situation in which you are directly affected by the behavior of your coworker, for example, she is late in relieving you from your shift, she is not doing her fair share in a joint project, or she is having loud and distracting conversations in the cubicle next to yours, there is always justification for having the difficult conversation yourself. However, it is also quite possible that there is someone else who should have the conversation with her, namely your boss. Unfortunately, there is no hard-and-fast rule, and a lot depends on the character of your boss and the coworker. If your boss cannot be relied on to have the difficult conversation on your behalf, then you have to have the difficult conversation yourself. If you have tried to have the conversation with your coworker and nothing changes, then you may decide to get your boss involved.

In these three examples, let's consider the questions we posed in chapter 2: Does policy require that I have this conversation? Am I directly affected by or involved in the issue? And is there someone else who should have this conversation? Policy will only very occasionally have a role to play in coworker conversations. The second question is more obvious—you are directly impacted by your colleague's loud, personal conversations or their angry e-mail or a missed deadline. Finally, though your boss could be asked to have any of these conversations, you will be more likely to make progress with the situation by approaching your colleague directly since you are the one who is witnessing and experiencing the problematic behavior.

The point to keep in mind is that you need to get clear: whether you end up having the conversation yourself or passing the responsibility onto someone else, you need to make the decision after careful thought. This is in contrast to just acting without getting clear first. If you don't take the time to consider the questions we present here, you may end up having a difficult conversation you didn't need to have, or one that proves ineffective.

Other examples involving coworkers include: "I notice that you leave the microwave dirty" and "I notice that you are coming in late to work." These are examples of conversations that are not yours to have. These examples fail the three-question test: there is no policy requiring you to have the conversation, you are not directly affected by the behavior (you are only affected tangentially), and there is someone else who should have the conversation, namely the boss.

Conversely, there are certain coworker situations that *are* your conversations to have. Or, at least, the answers to the three questions are not so cut and dried. First, consider the example of two coworkers who are working on a project together and neither thinks the other is doing their fair share. This time, however, *you* are one of those coworkers and not just a disinterested third party. Then this is a conversation that you need to have because you are directly affected by the behavior. Similarly, if you work a service desk shift and the coworker who is supposed to relieve you is chronically late, this is another example of when you might need to have the difficult conversation yourself. Finally, if a coworker sends an e-mail that seems angry in tone, then you will likely need to have this difficult conversation yourself.

GATHERING DOCUMENTATION

As discussed in chapter 3, this is the opportunity to consider what documentation you might gather that would be helpful in the conversation you are contemplating. In the situation where you are approaching a coworker about his loud personal conversations in a cubicle environment, no documentation may be available. However, in a situation where a colleague sends you an e-mail that appears angry, a copy of the e-mail will be useful to bring to the conversation. Additionally, with the example of you and a colleague working together on a project, there could be meeting minutes that you can refer to in the conversation to remind both of you what was agreed upon at the last meeting. Printing out copies of e-mails and meeting minutes can help guide a conversation and keep it focused on the facts of the situation rather than your potential irritation.

CLARIFYING YOUR MESSAGE

Now let's consider each of these three situations of coworker issues as you clarify your message by focusing on the facts of the situation, the expectations you have for your colleague's behavior, and developing your 3 × 5 card.

Ex: 1 You and Eleanor and Loud Conversations

The facts: Eleanor has loud, personal conversations on her cell phone with her mother, who is hard of hearing and who was recently relocated to an assisted-living arrangement. And you and Eleanor have office space next to each other in a cubicle environment, so her loud conversations are easy to hear and very distracting.

Even though you may have opinions about the fact that Eleanor is using work time for personal business, the behavior you really want to stop is her making the calls from her cubicle. You would like to ask Eleanor to step outside of the cubicle area when she makes personal calls.

The 3 × 5 card might look like this:

- Loud, personal conversations are distracting
- I'm concerned about you *and* I need to get work done
- I would like you to take the phone calls outside of the office suite

Ex: 2 You and Maria and the Angry E-Mail

The facts: you sent an e-mail to Maria as an informational item to make sure she was in the loop and knew she could attend an upcoming meeting if she wanted. Maria sent an e-mail in reply that had "?!" in the Subject line of the e-mail. Though the content of Maria's e-mail included a number of questions, the overall tone appeared angry because of the Subject line. Your expectation is that if Maria is upset by something you said in your e-mail she will come to you in person to talk it out. The 3 × 5 card might look like this:

- Your e-mail seemed angry
- I care about our ability to work together so I want to clear this up
- I would like you to come to me in person to talk over something if you are upset

Ex: 3 You and Erik and the Subject Guide

The facts: you and Erik are working on a joint subject guide on resources for innovators and entrepreneurs. You bring the engineering background and Erik has the business resources. At your last meeting, you and Erik had agreed upon a common deadline for selecting and describing the databases that would appear in that section of the subject guide. Your databases are on the draft guide, but Erik has missed the deadline. The 3×5 card might look like this:

- We agreed to have our databases on the draft guide by July 12
- Your databases are not on the draft guide
- I would like your databases to be on the draft guide during the next week to keep the project moving forward

CONNECTING THE CONVERSATION WITH THE WRITE-UP

With a coworker, the beginning of a difficult conversation will likely have a preamble that is not necessary with an employee. We recommend beginning by asking your coworker if she has a couple of minutes to talk. If she says "yes," you can get right to the facts of the situation. If she says "no," we recommend trying to find a common time that would work later in the day.

We have found that with coworkers there is an added temptation to put off the conversation. We encourage you to have difficult conversations with coworkers sooner rather than later to avoid building up resentments, especially in cases where your coworker is doing something especially annoying or has indicated nonverbally or in writing that she is angry with you. Putting off a conversation will only increase your irritation or heighten anxiety when you are around your coworker.

As you might imagine, a write-up of a conversation with a coworker is going to be even more informal than a write-up of a conversation with someone you supervise. Your notes will require a great deal more finesse and a focus on thanking the other person, assuming that the conversation went well.

We will take each example in turn to demonstrate the use of the steps during the conversation and the write-up afterwards.

Ex: 1 You and Eleanor and Loud Conversations

You: Can I talk to you for a couple of minutes? I need to chat about something and it really will only take a few minutes.

Eleanor: Sure. What's up?

The rest of the conversation follows the steps outlined in chapter 5 and could go something like this:

You: I've been noticing recently that you have had several personal phone calls during which you talk loud enough that I can easily hear you in my cubicle. I don't want to eavesdrop, but you talk loud enough that I have no way to keep from hearing it. First, are you okay? Is there anything I can do to help?

Note: This statement of concern will disarm someone who is ready to be defensive or angry or may just be completely stressed out. However, this kind of question may lead to a long story, which will require patience on your side. If you don't care what your colleague may or may not be going through and don't have the patience to listen to her story, consider making a statement of concern rather than asking a question. For example,

You: The conversations sound really rough and I feel terrible for you, and I'm also really struggling to concentrate while you're in the middle of those conversations.

Eleanor: I'm so sorry. I didn't realize that I was being that loud. My mother is hard of hearing so I have to talk louder than usual so she can hear me. I can easily take these calls outside of our office area.

You: Thank you so much! That will really help me. I also appreciate being able to have this conversation with you. I know conversations like this are awkward, but I value being able to work with you. If there is ever anything you need to talk with me about, I hope you'll do that.

The notes for this conversation will often take the form of a simple "thank you" note and a reiteration of your appreciation of the coworker's willingness to adjust. It could look something like this:

> **Date:** Thursday, May 26, 2016 at 8:58 PM
> **From:** You
> **To:** Eleanor Schmidt < eleanor.schmidt@public_library.org >
> **Subject:** Thank you

Hi Eleanor,

Thanks so much for our quick chat today. I wanted to say again how much I appreciate your willingness to take your phone calls outside of the office area. It's so important to me to be able to talk about these small things so they don't become large things that interrupt our ability to work together, and I especially appreciate your willingness to join me in that conversation.

Please know that I'm just as willing to have this kind of conversation with you if there is something I'm doing that is bothersome.

Again, thank you for being such a great colleague.

Ex: 2   You and Maria and the Angry E-Mail

You: Can I talk to you for a couple of minutes? I need to chat about something and it really will only take a few minutes.

Maria: Sure. What's up?

You: I got your e-mail this morning in response to mine and it seemed angry. I got concerned because I appreciate our working relationship and want to see that continue. Are you angry about my e-mail?

Maria: Did I sound angry? What did I say?

You: Well, the thing that seemed angry was the "?!" in the Subject line of the e-mail.

Maria: Did I put a "?!" in the Subject line? I didn't mean to do that! How weird. I'm not at all angry. I had some questions, but I didn't intend for the e-mail to sound angry.

You: Well, that's a relief! You know, if you ever *are* upset about something I do or say, I hope you'll stop by and talk to me about it. I'm really open to hearing that kind of thing. Keeping a good working relationship is important to me and I would rather have an awkward conversation than have resentments build up.

Again, the write-up for this conversation will be more in the form of a "thank you":

Date: Thursday, July 21, 2016 at 4:32 PM
From: You
To: Maria Rodriguez < maria.rodriguez@public_library.org >
Subject: Thank you

Hi Maria,

Thanks so much for our quick chat today. I'm so glad to hear that you aren't angry and I'll take a minute tomorrow to answer the questions you have in the e-mail. I wanted to say again how much I appreciate being able to have this conversation with you and your willingness to talk to me directly about anything that is bothering you. It's so important to me to be able to talk about these small things so they don't become large things that interrupt our ability to work together, and I especially appreciate your willingness to join me in that conversation.

Please know that I'm just as willing to have this kind of conversation with you if there is something I'm doing that is bothersome.

Again, thank you for being such a great colleague.

Ex: 3 You and Erik and the Subject Guide

In this example, you will have to make a decision about when to hold the conversation. Is there a regular meeting coming up soon? If so, then waiting for that regular meeting is a good choice. If the next meeting isn't for a while, we recommend setting a meeting to discuss the missed deadline following the recommendations in chapter 2 under the heading, "How do you schedule this conversation?"

You: Thanks for meeting me, Erik. I wanted to go over the project plan and the deadlines to make sure we're on track. When I checked the draft subject guide yesterday, I didn't see your databases on there. We had talked about having our databases on the draft guide on Tuesday. Did something happen?

Erik: Yeah, sorry I missed the deadline, I just got behind and had an unexpected class to teach. You would think that wouldn't happen very much during the summer, but a faculty member asked me to teach his class at the last minute.

You: Got it. That makes sense. We have a number of other sections to fill out on the subject guide before fall semester starts. Do you think you can put your databases up there sometime next week?

Erik: Oh yes. I should be able to get them up there by tomorrow, Friday.

You: Great! Let's talk about the next steps too, since we're here and make sure we are on target.

Your write-up of the conversation will be in the form of meeting notes and include anything you agreed to do, anything Erik agreed to do, and the dates by which each of you will get these things completed.

Date: Thursday, July 14, 2016 at 4:32 PM
From: You
To: Erik Hoffman < erik.hoffman@public_library.org >
Subject: Meeting Notes—July 14

Hi Erik,

Thanks for meeting today. Here are my notes and action items from our meeting. Would you let me know by Monday, July 18 if I misunderstood anything? Thanks!

We are making good progress on the new subject guide. We agreed to create a tab of resources that will include ourselves and other librarians whose subjects connect in some way to innovation. We also agreed to move Marketing to the last tab since that would generally come at the end of a project.

Action Items for you:
- Databases up on the draft guide by tomorrow, July 15
- Marketing resources in the marketing tab by next week, July 22
- Action Items for me:
- Select and add the most pivotal engineering books, both e-books and print by next week, July 22
- Set the next meeting for our project.

Thanks again for meeting!

A NOTE ON RESENTMENTS

When it comes to our coworkers, our usual advice to avoid difficult conversations unless they are absolutely necessary does not work as well. In fact, we would frequently give exactly the opposite advice if the difficult conversation needs to be with a colleague. Conflict with our colleagues has the tendency to fester into resentments and coalitions, both of which tend to be more destructive to ourselves and our work environment than what might be obvious at the beginning of a resentment.

Self-righteous anger is delicious. It is what frequently fuels a resentment against someone else. The belief, even the knowledge, that someone else hurt me, slighted me, or did something wrong to me or others is a sure way to begin a resentment. This kind of thinking frequently leads to long-standing resentments and avoidance of another person, and brings a temporary feeling of empowerment through anger. What is less understood is that when we hold a resentment, it actually causes much more damage to us than the other person. The other person may be blissfully unaware of our anger and they are going along in their life without thinking about us at all. Meanwhile, we are steeped in anger, bitterness, disappointment, and obsessive thoughts of what this other person did. This takes up a lot of mental space and can ruin our days, weeks, and months if we continue to hold onto this anger. It saps our energy, impairs our usual good mood, and can destroy our otherwise good feelings about our workplace. And yet, the satisfaction of self-righteous anger coupled with the fear of having a difficult conversation can keep us caught in this trap.

Hosting a difficult conversation to clear up what happened, to ask questions, or to understand what another person might be thinking or dealing with can restore order and harmony. However, we must be brave enough to take the action of holding a difficult conversation. This brings us back to the beginning of the process outlined in this book for holding difficult conversations. Getting clear about your role in the situation is imperative before moving forward.

What if you determine that this is not a conversation you should be having, but you are still angry? Or what if you hold a difficult conversation with another person who doesn't want to participate in the conversation? You are left holding the bag of your anger and resentment. What now?

The only person we can change in this world is ourselves, so you are left to consider doing some internal work. Whenever you have thoughts about the situation that is bothering you, take some time to wish the other person well. Wish them health, happiness, peace, and prosperity or whatever it is you wish for yourself. You are not doing this for the other person's sake, you are doing this for you. You are establishing your peace of mind, your health and well-being, so that years from now you are not the angry, bitter person whom everyone wishes would retire. It sounds ridiculous to wish someone well who has hurt you, who you would prefer to avoid, and frankly, is someone you just don't like. Your commitment to your peace of mind and your own health and well-being has to be your top priority in order for this to work. When we have attempted this process, we found that initially we didn't mean the well-wishes and often said them through gritted teeth. Over time, however, the anger diminished and resentments faded. The other person frequently remains blissfully unaware of any of this, so the removal of resentments is a gift we give to ourselves.

Careful consideration and preparation should accompany any difficult conversation, and the steps are largely the same with coworkers as they are with employees, with some adjustments. Having the skills to manage a difficult conversation with a colleague is the key to your own integrity and peace of mind.

CHAPTER NINE

A Brief Note about Change Management

I **N THIS CHAPTER, WE WILL USE THE TOOLS DESCRIBED IN** earlier chapters in the context of change management. Since libraries rely heavily on technology and technology is changing rapidly, libraries must adjust quickly to keep up with the technology that we use and the technology that our customers are using. We use strategic planning as a mechanism to learn where our libraries currently are and where we want to go. These strategic planning moments are often followed by a reorganization of personnel to better situate staff to meet the goals just set. Learning how to help people through strategic planning and reorganization is imperative to its success. However, it will most likely require many difficult conversations.

By way of background, there is a growing body of literature describing mechanisms to plan and implement change throughout an organization. Several books and articles that have been useful to the authors discuss change management in a variety of contexts: in higher education (Eckel, Green, Hill, and Mallon 1999), nonprofit organizations (Hanleybrown, Kania, and Kramer 2012), and business (Kotter 1995; Judge and Terrell 2013). In addition, there are definitely articles that discuss change management in libraries (Chamberlain and Reece 2014; Channing 1999; Ellis, Rosenblum, Stratton, and Ames-Stratton 2014; Franklin 2009; Heinrich, Helfer, and Woodley 2009; and Schwartz 1997).

Though these articles and books on change management are excellent reference tools, there are two components they rarely address: how to handle employees who resist change, and how to hold others and ourselves accountable for implementing the change.

RESISTANCE AND ACCOUNTABILITY

1 Resistance to Change

As for the first component, dealing with resisters to change, much of the literature on organizational change speaks about the fact that there will be resistance to change. However, there is very little written on how to address this reality. Books and articles warn us of trouble ahead, but rarely equip us to handle it. As mentioned in the first chapter, a typical difficult conversation can center on telling someone to do something they don't want to do or telling someone that you need them to stop doing something they like to do. When you implement organizational change, the number of people you need to tell to do things they don't want to do or to stop doing things they like to do increases dramatically. In fact, it is possible that during an organizational change, a large group of employees will only hear the words "Start doing this, and stop doing that," to the exclusion of all else.

Many of our examples throughout this book focused heavily on telling employees to "stop doing something," for example, stop being late, stop banging your fist on the table, and so on. Now we would like to focus on telling people to do something that they really don't want to do.

2 Accountability

As for the second component, holding others and ourselves accountable, the literature on organizational change provides useful steps to follow, but often does not address how to hold others and ourselves accountable to make the changes that are being asked of us. Chapter 6 provides guidance on holding people accountable by writing up the content of a conversation, including agreements by both parties. This same mechanism works well during organizational change and managing the resulting resistance.

The key to both of these issues and so many others is holding effective difficult conversations. Our organizations are made up of individuals. In order to move an organization toward a vision of a new tomorrow you need to focus on the big picture, set goals, and create a common vision. It also demands focusing on the individual through one-on-one conversations, especially when there is resistance.

TWO EXAMPLES

Ex: 1 Harry and Stan

Let's take the example of a library that has a goal of improving communication throughout the organization. Librarians and staff were especially insistent on improved communication about progress made on technology problems. In applying this goal to his unit, the Information Technology (IT) manager, Harry, presented an initial question to his group of employees as to how they thought they might improve communication during their everyday work. As the group discussed possibilities, there was some consensus, though not unanimous agreement, that sending e-mail to a user within twenty-four hours of the receipt of a request seemed like a good place to start. A few of the IT professionals were unhappy about this change, since stopping their work to send e-mail would just slow down the process of fixing what was wrong. Stan, a direct report to Harry, was having an especially difficult time accepting this change. Since user requests are submitted through an automated system, Harry could see that Stan was not consistently sending a reply to a request for assistance in the agreed-upon twenty-four hours. Out of 20 requests for help over the past two weeks, Stan had sent only 5 replies to requests within 24 hours. The rest of the requests remained open and unanswered.

To begin, Harry answered the questions posed in chapter 2. First, Harry recognized his role as a supervisor and realized that this was his conversation to have. Second, he had provided sufficient time to establish a pattern and felt that dealing with the situation soon after this realization would be better. Finally, he knew that if he didn't have this conversation that the behavior would continue.

The documentation Harry decided to bring to the meeting with Stan included the log of the technology help requests over the past two weeks, including those that Stan responded to and those that remained unanswered.

As Harry was clarifying his message, he created a 3×5 card that looked something like this:

- Agreement about sending an e-mail within twenty-four hours after receipt of a request for help.
- Reviewed two weeks of logs and noticed that of the 20 requests that came to Stan, only 5 were sent e-mails.
- How can we work together to meet the organizational and unit goal?

Harry felt ready for the conversation, so he sent an e-mail to Stan on Tuesday morning, June 21, asking to meet at 3:00 p.m. to review the log of requests for help. Since Stan worked in a cubicle environment, Harry asked Stan to come to Harry's office so their conversation could remain private. In preparation for that meeting, Harry cleaned off the small table in his office and placed the log with requests for help on the table.

Harry: Thanks for coming to meet with me, Stan. Have a seat. I wanted to talk with you about the agreement that the group made three weeks ago that we began implementing on June 6. We agreed to send an e-mail within twenty-four hours of receiving a request for help. I reviewed these logs and noticed that you did respond to some people within twenty-four hours, but a majority still have not received an e-mail from you. Can you tell me your thoughts about this? Was there a reason that five people got a response, but the others didn't?

Stan: Well, yeah, I was able to fix the problem with those 5 within 24 hours, so I let them know that I fixed their problem. I'm still working on the other ones.

Harry: That's great that you were able to fix those five problems so quickly, and it's really important that you communicate with the other fifteen people that you are still working on their issues.

Stan: Well, if I take time to send them e-mail, I'm losing that time when I could be working to fix their problems. Don't you think they want me to fix their computers faster?

Harry: I'm not saying that I don't want you to fix their computer problems quickly. I am saying that I want you to send e-mail to each person within twenty-four hours of receipt of their request for help. Is there some way we can work together on this? For example, if you are convinced that people don't care if you respond to them within twenty-four hours and would rather have you focus on fixing the problem, is there a way to evaluate that assumption?

Stan: I don't know. I just know that if I spend time sending e-mail, I'm not spending time fixing the problem.

Harry: We have an assessment librarian whose specialty is to collect data on this exact kind of thing and analyze that data to help us answer questions. Would you be willing to work with me and her to create an assessment project?

Stan: I'll come to whatever meeting you want me to go to.

Harry: Do you have any suggestions about how to fix this gap between the agreement of an e-mail in twenty-four hours and your inconsistency in doing so?

Stan: Nope.

Harry: Alright. Well, how about this? Right now, you are answering people right away 25 percent of the time. Let's aim for progress over the next few weeks by increasing that percentage. Over the next two weeks, I would like you to e-mail 50 percent of the requests for help within twenty-four hours. Then, let's meet and see how that went. It's just 5 more e-mails if 20 requests are a typical amount of requests in a two-week time period. Does that sound fair?

Stan: Sure. But I really think people would rather that I just fix their computer problems.

Harry: You may be right. I'll set up a meeting with Suzanne, the assessment librarian, and we'll create a study to double-check that assumption.

Stan: Fine.

Harry: Thanks for meeting with me, Stan. I'll also set up another meeting in two weeks to see how things are going.

After this meeting, Harry's meeting notes looked like this:

Date: Wednesday, June 22, 2016 at 8:58 PM
From: Harry Porter < harry.porter@public_library.org >
To: Stan Sternhouse < stan.sternhouse@public_library.org >
Subject: Meeting Notes from 6/21/2016

Hi Stan,
Thanks for meeting with me yesterday. I thought it would be helpful to send some notes after the meeting to make sure we are both on the same page.

We talked about the agreement from the IT Group where we agreed to send e-mail to each user who requested technology help within 24 hours. I noticed over the past two weeks that you had sent 5 e-mails to users who requested help within 24 hours, but the other 15 requests did not receive an e-mail response from you in that 24-hour time frame. You said that you were able to fix the problem with those 5 within 24 hours, so you sent them e-mail, but the other ones you're still working on. You also suggested that by sending e-mail responses, you are using time to send e-mail instead of fixing the problem and that people would prefer that you fix their computer problems faster. I suggested that we test those assumptions by inviting the assessment librarian to help us develop a way to collect data and analyze the results. Meanwhile, you agreed to increase the percentage of people you e-mail within 24 hours of receipt of their request for help to 50 percent over the next two weeks.

I agreed to set up another meeting for us in two weeks to see how this is going. I also agreed to set up a meeting with Suzanne Sager, the assessment librarian, and the two of us to begin a conversation about an assessment project.

Please let me know if I misunderstood anything and send me corrections to these notes by Friday, June 25.

Thanks!
Harry

Ex: 2   Yolanda and Hector

Another example resulting from organizational change might be an academic library whose public services group has decided on a new model of reference service. Statistics gathered at the reference desk indicated a drop in the number of questions and an increase in simple questions that did not require the expertise of a librarian. A survey of faculty provided data that showed a majority of faculty getting their library resources from their offices. Finally, the number of online courses and completely online programs offered by the university had increased dramatically over the past year, with plans for continuing that trajectory. This had an effect on the demand for chat reference, increasing the number of questions coming in by 50 percent.

As a result, the group decided that instead of spending time staffing a reference desk, librarians should connect with faculty in their offices rather than expecting faculty to come to the library for assistance. The group further decided that the reference desk should become an information desk staffed with professional staff and hourly student employees. The information desk personnel would provide referrals to librarians when needed. Additionally, it was decided that chat reference should be staffed by librarians and professional staff during all the hours the library was open.

Yolanda was the supervisor for seven librarians, all of who participated in the above discussions. Though a majority agreed with the new direction, there were a couple of librarians who strongly disagreed. Hector, one of Yolanda's direct reports, remained convinced that moving librarians away from the reference desk was a huge mistake. Furthermore, he struggled to embrace new technology and software and though he was capable of making a change to new software, he would do so at a slower pace than his colleagues.

The chat reference coordinator, Ramona, sent out a request to librarians to sign up for chat reference shifts. She encouraged everyone to take two shifts of two hours each with a due date of August 1, since she was preparing the schedule for the fall semester. After the deadline had passed, Ramona sent reminder messages to those who had not responded. By Thursday, August 4, Ramona had not heard from Hector, so she set up a meeting with Hector's supervisor to see if Yolanda would have better luck.

After the meeting, Yolanda began to answer the questions posed in chapter 2. Was this her conversation to have? Yolanda had to admit that Ramona had done what was expected in her role as coordinator to get a response from Hector. Since Yolanda was Hector's supervisor, that would make the next conversation one that she should have.

Why would Yolanda need to have this conversation now? The timing was short because the fall semester was to start in another couple of weeks, so having the conversation sooner rather than later would be beneficial. And Yolanda knew that if she didn't have this conversation, then Hector would not sign up for any chat reference shifts. While that wasn't the end of the world, it was a significant departure from his colleagues and their agreed-upon new direction. Since this was a Friday afternoon, Yolanda thought it would be better to wait for Monday, August 8, to hold the meeting.

Yolanda asked Ramona for the online schedule for chat reference and the e-mails asking for participation, which she had sent to the group and to

Hector individually. Yolanda planned to bring that documentation to the meeting with Hector.

Yolanda clarified her message and created a 3 × 5 card that looked something like this:

- Agreement about two shifts on chat reference
- Reviewed the chat reference schedule and noticed that Hector's name was not present
- I wonder what is keeping Hector from participating

As part of this step, Yolanda had to take into account that prior to being Hector's supervisor, they were once just equal colleagues. Hector had reached out to Yolanda when she was new to the job and the city and had invited her to meet his family and friends. They had spent several holidays together during those first ten years and Yolanda had attended many family celebrations as well. As Yolanda became Hector's supervisor, they continued to socialize with those same people who were now mutual friends and Yolanda had grown quite close to Hector's oldest daughter. Yolanda worried that this difficult conversation would ruin the friendship between her and Hector and his oldest daughter. Hector's oldest daughter would soon be having her first child and Yolanda had been invited to a baby shower on August 13.

As a result, Yolanda revisited her earlier decision about the timing of the conversation. If she had the conversation on Monday, August 8, that could make the baby shower very uncomfortable. However, the business need was to have a schedule in place for the fall semester, and if the conversation didn't happen this week, it would be too late to correct. Yolanda stayed with her initial instincts to have the conversation on Monday and hoped that she could find a mutually beneficial solution.

On Monday morning, Yolanda sent an e-mail to Hector asking him to meet with her on Monday afternoon at 1:30 p.m. to talk about the chat reference schedule. Since Hector had an office with a door, Yolanda thought it might be less threatening if she held the meeting in Hector's office. Hector agreed.

Yolanda: Hi Hector. Thanks for meeting with me. Knowing that we just recently had a meeting where the overall public services group decided on a different reference model, I decided to review the chat reference schedule to see how it was working out. I noticed your name was not on the schedule. Was that a mistake?

Hector: No, no, that wasn't a mistake. I just didn't sign up.

Yolanda: Can you tell me why?

Hector: Well, all the open times conflicted with classes I usually teach. And what is the point anyway? Chat is a horrible way to provide reference services. There's no way to see the other person's body language to see if they understand or if they still have questions. How can you hold a reference interview over chat?

Yolanda: Ok, I'm hearing two things. First, that there were a lot of conflicts with the chat schedule and your teaching schedule, and I have a sense that there would be a way to work that out by talking with Ramona. We used to do that with the reference desk schedule and it seemed to work fine. Second, I'm hearing that you can't imagine conducting a reference interview using chat and that there are limitations inherent in not being able to see the person who is asking for help. Is that about right?

Hector: Yes, I completely disagree with using chat as a way to provide reference. There's just no way to provide a good reference interview!

Yolanda: What's hard to ignore is that chat statistics have grown over the past year as have online courses. Some of our students won't be able to reach us any other way and still more don't want to talk to us in person. Ramona and others held training sessions and created a best practices document to guide librarians to provide exceptional service over chat. There are ways to get around some of the limitations that chat has. Have you been to any of the chat training sessions?

Hector: I'm a busy man. I didn't have time to attend those sessions so I don't know how to work chat.

Yolanda: Not knowing how is something that can be fixed! Maybe there is some way we can find some middle ground that would provide some training before taking on a full shift? For example, since chat tends to be slow until the fall break, would you be willing to get individual training from Ramona and observe her and others do their chat shifts instead of having a shift of your own? Then after fall break, you could take on your own two-hour shift. Does that sound fair?

Hector: I don't like that Ramona. She's bossy.

Yolanda: Ok, how about working with Michael?

Hector: Yeah, okay. I could work with Michael.

Yolanda: Ok, here's what I'll do. I'll e-mail Ramona with a copy to you letting her know the plan and to schedule you on chat after fall break, meaning after October 16. Then I'll e-mail Michael, also with a copy to you, and ask him to provide you the chat training and then allow you to shadow him on his chat shift. I think it would be helpful to shadow him at least three times. What do you think? Is three times enough?

Hector: Yes, I think that would be enough, but I'm still not happy about using chat reference.

Yolanda: I can hear that you are still unhappy and that concerns me. You are someone I trust and care about and I hate having to insist, but this is the direction the group agreed upon and I have to make sure everyone is doing their part. That's why I wanted to have a conversation with you directly. I respect you too much to just send e-mail. You deserve the respect of me coming to your office to try to work this out. And I really appreciate that you are willing to meet me part way.

Hector: Thank you. I do appreciate that respect.

Yolanda: You and I have regular meetings, so let's make this a topic of conversation as we meet through the semester. I'll be interested in hearing how the training is going and how your first several shifts work out. Thanks again, Hector.

After this conversation, Yolanda's meeting notes looked like this:

Date: Tuesday, August 9, 2016 at 2:45 PM
From: Yolanda Williams <yolanda.williams@univ.edu>
To: Hector Brown <hector.brown@univ.edu>
Subject: Meeting Notes from August 8

Hi Hector,

Thanks again for meeting with me yesterday. Here's what I think we talked about and what we each agreed to do. Would you look it over and let me know if I misunderstood anything by Thursday, August 11? Thanks for helping me keep us on the same page!

We talked about the chat reference schedule for the fall semester and the fact that you hadn't signed up to take any shifts. After a brief conversation, one of the reasons you were hesitant to sign up was that you didn't know how to use chat. You were agreeable to using the first portion of the fall semester for training and then to take on a chat shift after fall break.

I agreed to send e-mail to Ramona with a copy to you to let her know this plan and to work with you to find a two-hour chat reference shift for you to take after October 16.

I agreed to send e-mail to Michael with a copy to you to ask him to provide training and at least three opportunities for you to shadow him while he was answering chat reference questions. Once you and Michael receive that e-mail, I'll expect you to take the lead to arrange the training and shadowing sessions.

Thanks again, Hector, for meeting with me and working this out. Our next regular meeting is scheduled for August 24. Thanks also for sending me any edits to these notes by Thursday, August 11, if I got something wrong.

Warm regards,
Yolanda

Change is hard on everyone throughout an organization. Those who invoke change often worry if the organization will be able to recover and move forward. Those upon whom change is inflicted may not feel appreciated or valued if their particular recommendation was not followed. They may feel uncertain about their new roles or the new tasks they have been asked to do. This might be an especially disturbing feeling for those who have been working in the field of librarianship for many years. Acquiring the skill to approach each person with a statement of facts, compassion for the other person, and a frame of mind that encourages success can ease what otherwise might be a particularly difficult transition.

CHAPTER TEN

Managing Up
How to Have Difficult Conversations with Your Boss

M ANY OF US HAVE EXPERIENCED A VARIETY OF BOSSES. ALL OF them have provided excellent examples of leadership, some of which help us to see what works well, while others help us to see what we want to avoid. In either case, there will likely be a time when you need something from your supervisor. The book *Managing Up: Expert Solutions to Everyday Challenges* (2008) presents a few general points as a guide to having a difficult conversation with your boss:

1. *Connect your ideas to the goals of the organization and the goals of your boss.* People in leadership often need to speak with their upper administration about progress made by their unit toward organizational goals. Align your proposal with organizational goals or the goals your boss has set. This will help your boss look good in front of his bosses and can make your proposal more appealing.
2. *Provide actionable suggestions.* If you need to bring a problem to the attention of your boss, come prepared with at least one solution and how you will participate in making that solution come to life.

3. *Bring proposals that could help mitigate problems or reduce potential risks.*
   Imagine your boss wants to go down a path that you believe will reduce
   your unit's ability to provide the same level of excellent customer service
   as you have consistently provided in the past. Rather than dismiss your
   boss's vision entirely, describe the risks involved and provide another
   way to implement the vision without the loss of customer service.

4. *Provide alternative choices.* This is an especially effective tool to use when
   the situation is complex. Rearranging spaces in a library where offices
   may move and services may be consolidated is an opportunity to provide
   your boss with several scenarios and their benefits and difficulties to
   assist him with his decision making.

5 *Talk about your manager's concerns as part of your proposal.* As you present your new idea, consider using your supervisor's voiced concerns
   as a cornerstone of how your idea will help solve or lessen the concern.
   (33–34)

In our experience, it can be helpful to consider the personality of your boss. If
she is insecure, give her compliments before launching into a new proposal. If
she is a micromanager, give her frequent updates so she has a better idea of
what is going on. If she has a big ego and gets upset by your success, give her
a small credit for the work you accomplished by thanking her for whatever
she might have provided such as money, equipment, or space accompanied
by "I couldn't have done this without you." If your boss is more malleable
later in the week, arrange to have your meetings with her later in the week.
Consider your reality and adjust to meet that.

Another book by Gini Graham Scott, *A Survival Guide for Working with
Bad Bosses: Dealing with Bullies, Idiots, Back-Stabbers, and Other Managers from
Hell* (2006), has a chapter that recommends some personal reflection before
assuming that the problem resides entirely with your boss. Scott recommends
looking for patterns in your boss's behavior and asking, "Are you the only one
with the complaint?" If other colleagues have similar observations, they may
also have solutions that they have tried using with the boss more successfully.
If you seem to be the only one with a complaint, the problem might be you.
The book inspires even further reflection by encouraging us to ask how we
might have contributed to the situation in which we find ourselves. Is there
a way we might contribute to the solution? (177–81).

OTHER OPTIONS

There are times when despite your best efforts, you just simply do not get along with your boss. At that point you have a few options to consider:

- Get a new job and leave your current institution
- Get a new job within your current institution
- Stay in your current job for other reasons beyond total job satisfaction, such as loving where you live, proximity to family, your quality of life
- Stay in your current job in order to explore new areas of librarianship by lending a hand to a unit that is short-staffed or by getting more involved in professional organizations

The important aspect of this advice is that you must continue to build your resume and keep it up-to-date in order to have choices. If you are in academic libraries, this will mean publishing and presenting even if your current job does not demand it. If you do decide to stay in your current position, maintain a positive outlook and remain optimistic or risk becoming the bitter employee that no one wants to work with.

CONCLUSION

HOLDING DIFFICULT CONVERSATIONS IS A CONSISTENT PART OF our work lives. Learning how to manage these conversations well is imperative for both employees and those in leadership positions. When we can hold effective difficult conversations, it gives us a sense of integrity that we are doing the work we are getting paid to do and that we are doing it well. Rather than being a "mean" or "difficult" supervisor, we come to realize that holding an effective difficult conversation is one of the kindest, most compassionate things we can do. We empower ourselves and our colleagues to understand each other more thoroughly and to approach conflict with a sincere desire to work together.

Most libraries have a parent institution or are embedded in a larger organization. If we work for a public library, our funding frequently comes from the state legislature. The same is true if we work for a public university or college. If we work for a private company, there are shareholders to answer to. If we are at a private university or college, there are donors and governing bodies watching our work. Our ability to demonstrate that personnel issues are addressed quickly and effectively helps our ability to point to our overall success. It is difficult to overcome media stories about poor handling of personnel. These public statements, even if they are untrue, can lead state legislatures or shareholders or donors to wonder if they should be putting so much money into public education, or wonder why they are supporting public libraries or question the legitimacy of tenure. Our smaller moment of holding a difficult conversation has implications not only for the one or two people we are working with but also has huge ripple effects on our reputation as an organization and could influence the amount of money set aside for the work of our overall institutions and our library.

On the personal side, being brave enough to face another person, to say what needs to be said, and to respect the other person by listening carefully and working with her to meet common goals is a growth process. Gathering that courage again and again may initially appear daunting and leave you with a few sleepless nights. After you follow the steps described in this book on a regular basis, we hope you will agree that the benefit of overcoming that fear and going through the steps is completely worth it. Though at first these steps may seem cumbersome, once you apply them regularly, they will become your natural inclination. When thinking about an upcoming conversation, you will find yourself getting curious about the other person, how they see things, what is holding them back, what they are afraid of. You will get curious about yourself, wonder why you might be having a reaction to the behavior of a colleague and why that matters so much to you. As you see the positive results of your conversations by consistently applying the techniques in this book, you will gain courage and confidence both at work and in your personal life. We become better human beings and have more rewarding relationships by being able and willing to hold effective difficult conversations.

Though never easy, these conversations can be prepared for and can be productive. And, most importantly, you will gain confidence, strength, and integrity as you use these steps consistently with every difficult conversation.

REFERENCES

"Active Listening." BusinessDictionary. Alexandria, VA: Webfinance, Inc., May 22, 2016. www.businessdictionary.com/definition/active-listening.html.

Anderson, Janis F. "Teacher Immediacy as a Predictor of Teaching Effectiveness." In *Communication Yearbook 3,* edited by Dan Nimmo, 543–55. Thousand Oaks, CA: Sage, 1979.

Chamberlain, Clint, and Derek Reece. "Library Reorganization, Chaos, and Using the Core Competencies as a Guide." *The Serials Librarian* 66, no. 104 (2014): 248–52.

Channing, Rhoda. "Reorganization: The Next Generation." Presentation at the Association of College and Research Libraries Ninth National Conference, Detroit, MI, April 8–11, 1999.

Christophel, Diane M. "The Relationships among Teacher Immediacy Behaviors, Student Motivation, and Learning." *Communication Education* 39, no. 4 (1990): 323–40.

Eckel, Peter, Madeleine Green, Barbara Hill, and William Mallon. "On Change III–Taking Charge of Change: A Primer for Colleges and Universities." *An Occasional Paper Series of the ACE Project on Leadership and Institutional Transformation.* Washington, DC: American Council on Education, 1999.

Ellis, E. L., B. Rosenblum, J. M. Stratton, and K. Ames-Stratton. "Positioning Academic Libraries for the Future: A Process and Strategy for Organizational Transformation." Presentation at the International Association of Science and Technology Libraries Conference, Espoo, Finland, June 5, 2014.

Franklin, Brinley. "Aligning Library Strategy and Structure with the Campus Academic Plan: A Case Study." *Journal of Library Administration* 49, no. 5 (2009): 495–505.

Hanleybrown, Fay, John Kania, and Mark Kramer. "Channeling Change: Making Collective Impact Work." *Stanford Social Innovation Review* 20 (2012): 1–8.

Hattie, John, and Helen Timperley. "The Power of Feedback." *Review of Educational Research* 77, no. 1 (2007): 81–112.

Heinrich, Helen, Doris Helfer, and Mary Woodley. "Doing More with Less in Technical Services." *SEARCHER: The Magazine for Database Professionals,* July-August (2009): 7–9, 46.

Judge, William Q., and R. Steven Terrell. "Navigating the White Water of Organization Wide Change." In *Change Champion's Field Guide: Strategies and Tools for Leading Change in Your Organization,* 2nd edition, 51–72. Hoboken, NJ: John Wiley & Sons, 2013.

Kotter, John. "Leading Change: Why Transformation Efforts Fail." *Harvard Business Review,* March-April (1995): 59–67.

Managing Up: Expert Solutions to Everyday Challenges. Boston: Harvard Business Press, 2008.

Patterson, Kerry, Joseph Grenny, Ron McMillan, and Al Switzler. *Crucial Confrontations.* New York: McGraw-Hill, 2005.

Schwartz, Charles A. "Restructuring Academic Libraries: Adjusting to Technological Change." 1997. Association of College and Research Libraries. www.ala.org/acrl/publications/booksanddigitalresources/booksmonographs/pil/pi149/schwartzintro.

Scott, Gini Graham. *A Survival Guide for Working with Bad Bosses: Dealing with Bullies, Idiots, Back-Stabbers, and Other Managers from Hell.* New York: American Management Association, 2006.

Stone, Douglas, and Sheila Heen. *Thanks for the Feedback: The Science and Art of Receiving Feedback Well.* New York: Penguin, 2014.

INDEX

A

accountability and change management, 86–87

actionable suggestions, providing, 97

active listening, 44

agreement of action

    by employee included in your write-up of the conversation, 61–62

    by you included in your write-up of the conversation, 62–63

alternate choices, providing, 98

"always," avoiding the use of the word, 36

anger of other person in response to the conversation, 52–54

asking phrases used to invite the other person to talk about the situation, 38–39

B

boss, difficult conversations with. *See* managing up

C

change management

    accountability, 86–87

    articles and books on, 85–86

    overview, 85–86

    resistance to change, 86

change management examples

    communication improvement throughout organization example, 87–90

    documentation for conversation, 88, 91–92

    during the conversation, 88–89, 92–94

    need for conversation to be had by you, determining, 87, 91

    preparation for conversation, 88, 91–92

    reference service change example, 90–95

    write-up of conversation, 89–90, 94–95

clarifying the message

    to coworkers, 75–77

    emotions, filtering your, 29–31

    facts of the situation and expectations you have for your colleague's performance, focusing on, 27–29

    stating the facts, 34–38, 59–61

clarity on the situation. *See* self-reflection

clutter-free space, holding conversation in a, 49

collaboration with other person in conversation on solutions, 54–56

CPSIA information can be obtained
at www.ICGtesting.com
Printed in the USA
FFOW04n1353120518
46622722-48673FF